"A clearly written primer for the statistically impaired. It is as important to discussions of public policy as any book circulating today."

— *The Christian Science Monitor*

"Definitely a must for politicians, activists and others who generate or use statistics, but especially for those who want to think for themselves rather than take as gospel every statistic presented to them."

— *New Scientist*

"*Damned Lies and Statistics* is highly entertaining as well as instructive. Best's book shows how some of those big numbers indicating big social problems were created in the first place and instructs the reader (and reporter) how to be on guard against such gross manipulation. And it doesn't take an understanding of advanced mathematics to do so thanks to this book, which ought to be required reading in every newsroom in the country."

— *The Washington Times*

MORE DAMNED LIES AND STATISTICS

MORE DAMNED LIES AND STATISTICS

HOW NUMBERS CONFUSE PUBLIC ISSUES

JOEL BEST

UNIVERSITY OF CALIFORNIA PRESS
BERKELEY   LOS ANGELES   LONDON

University of California Press
Berkeley and Los Angeles, California

University of California Press, Ltd.
London, England

Library of Congress Cataloging-in-Publication Data

Best, Joel.
   More damned lies and statistics : how numbers confuse
public issues / Joel Best.
      p.   cm.
   Includes bibliographical references and index.
   ISBN 0–520–23830–3 (alk. paper).
      1. Sociology—Statistical methods.   2. Social problems—
Statistical methods.   3. Social indicators.   I. Title.

HM535.B474   2004
303.3'8—dc22   2003028076

Manufactured in the United States of America

13   12   11   10   09   08   07   06   05
10   9   8   7   6   5   4   3

Printed on Ecobook 50 containing a minimum 50% post-
consumer waste, processed chlorine free. The balance contains
virgin pulp, including 25% Forest Stewardship Council Certified
for no old growth tree cutting, processed either TCF or ECF. The
sheet is acid-free and meets the minimum requirements of
ANSI/NISO Z39.48–1992 (R 1997) (Permanence of Paper).

For Loy Bilderback

CONTENTS

ACKNOWLEDGMENTS

I had not planned to write this book. It is a sequel to my *Damned Lies and Statistics (DLS)*, which was published in 2001. When I finished writing *DLS*, I thought that I was through writing about statistics, and I had plans to begin working on a completely different project. Besides, I'm a professor, and professors don't get opportunities to write sequels—we feel fortunate if somebody is willing to publish, let alone read, what we write even once.

However, almost as soon as *DLS* appeared, I began getting e-mail messages from people who had read the book. Often, they drew my attention to wonderfully dubious statistics reported in the media. Among my favorites: a newspaper columnist who warned that smoking "kills one in five Americans each year"; and a British news item suggesting that "40 percent of young men have such a poor grasp of the way a bra fastens that they risk serious finger injuries." Others wrote to suggest topics that

DLS hadn't treated (some messages were from college instructors frustrated by the difficulties of conveying particular points in their courses).

I also began receiving invitations to talk to groups or write about statistics; often, I was asked to address particular topics that were not familiar to me. Studying new subjects sometimes raised new issues that I began to wish I'd addressed in *DLS*.

So when Naomi Schneider, my editor at the University of California Press, asked whether I might like to write a sequel to *DLS,* I agreed. I'd begun believing that I had enough ideas for another book, and there seemed to be enough people interested in the topic. I'm afraid I've lost track of the sources for some of my ideas, but I can at least thank those folks who I know made suggestions that were, in one way or another, incorporated in this book, along with thanking those who read and commented on parts of the manuscript. These include, in addition to Naomi, David Altheide, Ronet Bachman, Joan Best, George Bizer, Barbara Costello, Michael Gallagher, Linda Gottfredson, Larry Griffith, Henry Hipkens, Jim Holstein, Philip Jenkins, Vivian Klaff, the late Carl Klockars, Kathe Lowney, Katherine C. MacKinnon, Michael J. McFadden, Eric Rise, Naomi B. Robbins, Milo Schield, and—I fear—others whose names were inadvertently misplaced. I especially want to thank Vicky Baynes for helping me with the mysterious process of turning graphs into computer files. These people, of course, should be credited for providing help but not blamed for my interpretations. Thank you all. I hope this new book pleases you.

L unch was at a prominent conservative think tank. The people around the table were fairly well known; I'd read some of their books and articles and had even seen them interviewed on television. They listened to me talk about bad statistics, and they agreed that the problem was serious. They had only one major criticism: I'd missed the role of ideology. Bad statistics, they assured me, were almost always promoted by liberals.

Two months earlier, I'd been interviewed by a liberal radio talk-show host (they do exist!). He, too, thought it was high time to expose bad statistics—especially those so often circulated by conservatives.

When I talk to people about statistics, I find that they usually are quite willing to criticize dubious statistics—as long as the numbers come from people with whom they disagree. Political conservatives are convinced that the statistics presented by liberals are deeply flawed, just as liberals are eager to denounce conservatives' shaky figures. When conservatives (or liberals) ask me how to spot bad statistics, I suspect that they'd like me to say, "Watch out for numbers promoted by people with whom you disagree." Everyone seems to insist that the other guy's figures are lousy (but mine are, of course, just fine, or at least good enough). People like examples of an opponent's bad statistics, but they don't care to have their own numbers criticized because, they worry, people might get the wrong idea: criticizing my statistics might lead someone to question my larger argument, so let's focus on the other guy's errors and downplay mine.

Alas, I don't believe that any particular group, faction, or ideology holds a monopoly on poor statistical reasoning. In fact, in choosing examples to illustrate this book's chapters, I've tried to identify a broad range of offenders. My goal is not to convince you that those other guys can't be trusted (after all, you probably already believe that). Rather, I want you to come away from this book with a sense that all numbers—theirs and yours— need to be handled with care.

This is tricky, because we tend to assume that statistics are facts, little nuggets of truth that we uncover, much as rock collectors find stones.[1] After all, we think, a statistic is a number, and numbers seem to be solid, factual proof that someone must have actually counted something. But that's the point: people count. For every number we encounter, some person had to do the counting. Instead of imagining that statistics are like rocks, we'd do better to think of them as jewels. Gemstones may be found in nature, but people have to create jewels. Jewels must be selected, cut, polished, and placed in settings to be viewed from particular angles. In much the same way, people create statistics: they choose what to count, how to go about counting, which of the resulting numbers they share with others, and which words they use to describe and interpret those figures. Numbers do not exist independent of people; understanding numbers requires knowing who counted what, why they bothered counting, and how they went about it.

All statistics are products of social activity, the process sociologists call *social construction*. Although this point might seem painfully obvious, it tends to be forgotten or ignored when we think about—and particularly when we teach—statistics. We usually envision statistics as a branch of mathematics, a view reinforced by high school and college statistics courses, which begin by introducing probability theory as a foundation for statistical thinking, a foundation on which is assembled a structure of increasingly sophisticated statistical measures. Students are taught the underlying logic of each measure, the formula used to compute the measure, the software commands that can extract it from the computer, and some guidelines for interpreting the numbers that result from these computations. These are complicated lessons: few students have an intuitive grasp of any but the simplest statistics, and instruction usually focuses on clarifying the computational complexities.

The result is that statistical instruction tends to downplay consideration of how real-life statistics come into being. Yet all statistics are products of people's choices and compromises, which inevitably shape, limit, and distort the outcome. Statistics instructors often dismiss this as melodramatic irrelevance. Just as the conservatives at the think tank lunch imagined that bad statistics were the work of devious liberals, statistics instructors might briefly caution that calculations or presentations of statistical results may be "biased" (that is, intentionally designed to deceive). Similarly, a surprisingly large number of book titles draw a distinction between statistics and lies: *How to Lie with Statistics* (also, *How to Lie with Charts, How to Lie with Maps,* and so on); *How to Tell the Liars from the Statisticians; How Numbers Lie;* even (ahem) my own *Damned Lies and Statistics.*[2] One might conclude that statistics are pure, unless they unfortunately become contaminated by the bad motives of dishonest people.

Perhaps it is necessary to set aside the real world in an effort to teach students about advanced statistical reasoning. But dismissive warnings to watch out for bias don't go very far in preparing people to think critically about the numbers they read in newspaper stories or hear from television commentators. Statistics play important roles in real-world debates about social problems and social policies; numbers become key bits of evidence used to challenge opponents' claims and to promote one's own views. Because people do knowingly present distorted or even false figures, we cannot dismiss bias as nonexistent. But neither can we simply categorize numbers as either true figures presented by sincere, well-meaning people (who, naturally, agree with us) or false statistics knowingly promoted by devious folks (who are on the other side, of course).*

Misplaced enthusiasm is probably at least as common as deliberate bias in explaining why people spread bad statistics. Numbers rarely come first. People do not begin by carefully creating some bit of statistical information and then deduce what they ought to think. Much more often, they start with their own interests or concerns, which lead them to run across, or perhaps actively uncover, relevant statistical information. When these figures support what people already believe—or hope, or fear—to be true, it is very easy for them to adopt the numbers, to overlook or minimize their limitations, to find the figures first arresting, then compelling, and finally authoritative. People soon begin sharing these now important numbers with others and become outraged if their statistics are questioned. One need not intentionally lie to others, or even to oneself. One need only let down one's critical guard when encountering a number that seems appealing, and momentum can do the rest.

The solution is to maintain critical standards when thinking about statistics. Some people are adept at this, as long as they are examining their opponents' figures. It is much more difficult to maintain a critical stance toward our own numbers. After all, our numbers support what we believe to be true. Whatever minor flaws they might have surely must be unimportant. At least, that's what we tell ourselves when we justify having a double standard for judging our own statistics and those of others.

This book promotes what we might call a single standard for statistical criticism. It argues that we must recognize that all numbers are social products and that we cannot understand a statistic unless we know something about the process by which it came into being. It further argues that all statistics are imperfect and that we need to recognize and acknowledge their flaws and limitations. All this is true regardless of whether we agree or disagree with the people presenting the numbers. We need to think critically about both the other guys' figures and our own.

I should confess that, in writing this book, I have done little original research. I have borrowed most of my examples from works by other analysts, mostly social scientists and journalists. My goal in writing about bad statistics is to show how these numbers emerge and spread. Just as I do not believe that this is the work of one political faction, I do not mean to suggest that all the blame can be laid at the door of one segment of society, such as the media. The media often circulate bad numbers, but then so do activists, corporations, officials, and even scientists— in fact, those folks usually are the sources for the statistics that appear in the media. And, we should remember, the problems with bad statistics often come to light through the critical efforts of probing journalists or scientists who think the numbers through, discover their flaws, and bring those flaws to public attention. A glance at my sources will reveal that critical thinking, just like bad statistics, can be found in many places.

The chapters in this book explore some common problems in thinking about social statistics. The chapter titles refer to different sorts of numbers—missing numbers, confusing numbers, and so on. As I use them, these terms have no formal mathematical meanings; they are simply headings for organizing the discussion. Thus, chapter 1 addresses what I call *missing numbers,* that is, statistics that might be relevant to debates over social issues but that somehow don't emerge during those discussions. It identifies several types of missing numbers and seeks to account for their absence. Chapter 2 considers *confusing numbers,* basic problems that bedevil our understanding of many simple statistics and graphs. *Scary numbers*—statistics about risks and other threats—are the focus of chapter 3.

The next three chapters explore the relationship between authority and statistics. Chapter 4's subject is *authoritative numbers.* This chapter considers what we might think of as statistics that seem good enough to be beyond dispute—products of scientific research or government data collection, for instance. It argues that even the best statistics need to be handled with care, that even data gathered by experts can be subject to misinterpretation. Chapter 5 examines what I call *magical numbers*— efforts to resolve issues through statistics, as though figures are a way to distill reality into pure, incontrovertible facts. Chapter 6 concentrates on *contentious numbers,* cases of data duels and stat wars in which opponents hurl contradictory figures at one another. Finally, chapter 7 explores the prospects for teaching statistical literacy, for improving public understanding of numbers and teaching people how to be more thoughtful and more critical consumers of statistics.

The lesson that people count—that we don't just find statistics but that we create them—offers both a warning and a promise. The warning is that we must be wary, that unless we approach statistics with a critical attitude, we run the risk of badly misunderstanding the world around us. But there is also a promise: that we need not be at the mercy of numbers, that we can learn to think critically about them, and that we can come to appreciate both their strengths and their flaws.

C BS News anchor Dan Rather began his evening news-
cast on March 5, 2001, by declaring: "School shootings
in this country have become an epidemic." That day, a
student in Santee, California, had killed two other students and wounded thirteen more, and media coverage linked
this episode to a disturbing trend. Between December 1997 and
May 1998, there had been three heavily publicized school shooting incidents: in West Paducah, Kentucky (three dead, five
wounded); Jonesboro, Arkansas (five dead, ten wounded); and
Springfield, Oregon (two dead and twenty-one wounded at the
school, after the shooter had killed his parents at home). The following spring brought the rampage at Columbine High School
in Littleton, Colorado, in which two students killed twelve fellow students and a teacher, before shooting themselves.[1] Who
could doubt Rather's claim about an epidemic?

And yet the word *epidemic* suggests a widespread, growing

phenomenòn. Were school shootings indeed on the rise? Surprisingly, a great deal of evidence indicated that they were not:

· Since school shootings are violent crimes, we might begin by examining trends in criminality documented by the Federal Bureau of Investigation. The *Uniform Crime Reports,* the FBI's tally of crimes reported to the police, showed that the overall crime rate, as well as the rates for such major violent crimes as homicide, robbery, and aggravated assault, fell during the 1990s.

· Similarly, the National Crime Victimization Survey (which asks respondents whether anyone in their household has been a crime victim) revealed that victimization rates fell during the 1990s; in particular, reports of teenagers being victimized by violent crimes at school dropped.

· Other indicators of school violence also showed decreases. The Youth Risk Behavior Survey conducted by the U.S. Centers for Disease Control and Prevention found steadily declining percentages of high school students who reported fighting or carrying weapons on school property during the 1990s.

· Finally, when researchers at the National School Safety Center combed media reports from the school years 1992–1993 through 2000–2001, they identified 321 violent deaths that had occurred at schools. Not all of these incidents involved student-on-student violence; they included, for example, 16 accidental deaths and 56 suicides, as well as incidents involving nonstudents, such as a teacher killed by her estranged husband (who then shot himself) and a nonstudent killed on a school playground during a weekend. Even if we include all 321 of these deaths, however, the average fell from 48 violent deaths per year during the school years 1992–1993 through 1996–1997 to 32 per year from 1997–1998 through 2000–2001. If we eliminate accidental deaths and suicides, the decline remains, with the average falling from 31 deaths per year in the earlier period to 24 per year in the later period (which included all of the heavily publicized incidents mentioned earlier). While violent deaths are tragedies, they are also rare. Tens of millions of children attend school; for every million students, fewer than one violent death per year occurs in school.

In other words, a great deal of statistical evidence was available to challenge claims that the country was experiencing a sudden epidemic of school shootings. The FBI's *Uniform Crime Reports* and the National Crime Victimization Survey in particular are standard sources for reporters who examine crime trends; the media's failure to incorporate findings from these sources in their coverage of school shootings is striking.[2]

Although it might seem that statistics appear in every discussion of every social issue, in some cases—such as the media's coverage of school shootings—relevant, readily available statistics are ignored. We might think of these as *missing numbers*. This chapter examines several reasons for missing numbers, including overwhelming examples, incalculable concepts, uncounted phenomena, forgotten figures, and legendary numbers. It asks why potentially relevant statistics don't figure in certain public debates and tries to assess the consequences of their absence.

THE POWER OF EXAMPLES

Why are numbers missing from some debates over social problems and social policies? One answer is that a powerful example can overwhelm discussion of an issue. The 1999 shootings at Columbine High School are a case in point. The high death toll ensured that Columbine would be a major news story. Moreover, the school's location in a suburb of a major city made it easy for reporters to reach the scene. As it took some hours to evacuate the students and secure the building, the press had time to arrive and capture dramatic video footage that could be replayed to illustrate related stories in the weeks that followed. The juxtaposition of a terrible crime in a prosperous suburban community made the story especially frightening—if this school shooting could happen at Columbine, surely such crimes could happen anywhere. In addition, the Columbine tragedy occurred in the era of competing twenty-four-hour cable news channels; their decisions to run live coverage of several funeral and memorial services and to devote broadcast time to extended discussions of the event and its implications helped to keep the story alive for weeks.

For today's media, a dramatic event can become more than simply a news story in its own right; reporters have become attuned to searching for the larger significance of an event so that they can portray newsworthy incidents as instances of a widespread pattern or problem. Thus, Columbine, when coupled with the earlier, heavily publicized school shooting stories of 1997–1998, came to exemplify the problem of school violence. And, commentators reasoned, if a larger problem existed, it must reflect underlying societal conditions; that is, school shootings needed to be understood as a trend, wave, or epidemic with identifiable causes. Journalists have been identifying such crime waves since at least the nineteenth century—and, for nearly as long, criminologists have understood that crime waves are not so much patterns in criminal behavior as they are patterns in media coverage. All of the available statistical evidence suggested that school violence had declined from the early 1990s to the late 1990s; there was no actual wave of school shootings. But the powerful images from Columbine made that evidence irrelevant. One terrible example was "proof" that school shootings were epidemic.

Compelling examples need not even be true. The stories that folklorists call *contemporary legends* (or the more familiar term *urban legends*) also shape our thinking about social problems. Contemporary legends usually spread through informal channels, which once meant word of mouth but now also includes the more modern means of faxes and e-mail messages. A legend's key quality remains unchanged, however: it must be a good story, good enough for people to remember it and want to pass it along. Legends thrive because they arouse fear, disgust, or other powerful emotions that make the tales memorable and repeatable.[3] Very often, contemporary legends are topical: when child abductions are in the news, we tell stories about kidnappings in shopping malls; when gangs are receiving attention, we warn each other about lethal gang initiation rites. Such stories shape our thinking about social problems in much the same way dramatic news stories do.

The power of examples is widely recognized. A reporter preparing a story about any broad social condition—say, homelessness—is likely to begin by illustrating the problem with an example, perhaps a particular homeless person. Journalists (and their editors) prefer interesting, compelling examples that will intrigue their audience. And advocates who are trying to promote particular social policies learn to help journalists by guiding them to examples that can be used to make specific points.

Thus, activists calling for increased services for the homeless might showcase a homeless family, perhaps a mother of young children whose husband has been laid off by a factory closing and who cannot find affordable housing. In contrast, politicians seeking new powers to institutionalize the homeless mentally ill might point to a deranged, violent individual who seems to endanger passersby.[4] The choice of examples conveys a sense of a social problem's nature.

The problem with examples—whether they derive from dramatic events, contemporary legends, or the strategic choices of journalists or advocates—is that they probably aren't especially typical. Examples compel when they have emotional power, when they frighten or disturb us. But atypical examples usually distort our understanding of a social problem; when we concentrate on the dramatic exception, we tend to overlook the more common, more typical—but more mundane—cases. Thus, Democrats used to complain about Republican President Ronald Reagan's fondness for repeating the story of a "welfare queen" who had supposedly collected dozens of welfare checks using false identities.[5] Using such colorful examples to typify welfare fraud implies that welfare recipients are undeserving or don't really need public assistance. Defenders of welfare often countered Reagan's anecdotes with statistics showing that recipients were deserving (as evidenced by the small number of able-bodied adults without dependent children who received benefits) or that criminal convictions for fraud were relatively few.[6] The danger is that the powerful but atypical example—the homeless intact family, the welfare queen—will warp our vision of a social problem, thereby reducing a complicated social condition to a simple, melodramatic fable.

Statistics, then, offer a way of checking our examples. If studies of the homeless find few intact families (or individuals who pose threats of violence), or if studies of welfare recipients find that fraud involving multiple false identities is rare, then we should recognize the distorting effects of atypical examples and realize that the absence of numbers can damage our ability to grasp the actual dimensions of our problems.

THE INCALCULABLE

Sometimes numbers are missing because phenomena are very hard to count. Consider another crime wave. During the summer of 2002, public concern turned to kidnapped children. Attention first focused on the case of an adolescent girl abducted from her bedroom one night—a classic melodramatic example of a terrible crime that seemingly could happen to anyone. As weeks passed without a sign of the girl, both the search and the accompanying news coverage continued. Reports of other cases of kidnapped or murdered children began linking these presumably unrelated crimes to the earlier kidnapping, leading the media to begin talking about an epidemic of abductions.

This issue had a history, however. Twenty years earlier, activists had aroused national concern about the problem of missing children by coupling frightening examples to large statistical estimates. One widespread claim alleged that nearly two million children went missing each year, including fifty thousand kidnapped by strangers. Later, journalists and social scientists exposed these early estimates as being unreasonably high. As a result, in 2002, some reporters questioned the claims of a new abduction epidemic; in fact, they argued, the FBI had in-

vestigated more kidnappings the previous year, which suggested that these crimes were actually becoming less common.[7]

Both sets of claims—that kidnappings were epidemic and that
they were declining—were based on weak evidence. Missing-
children statistics can never be precise because missing children
are so difficult to count. We encounter problems of definition:

· What is a child—that is, what is the upper age limit for
being counted?

· What do we mean by missing? How long must a child be
missing to be counted—a few minutes, one day, seventy-two
hours?

· What sorts of absences should be counted? Wandering off
and getting lost? Running away? Being taken by a relative during a family dispute? Is a child who is with a noncustodial par-
ent at a known location considered missing?

People need to agree about what to count before they can start
counting, but not everyone agrees about the answers to these
questions. Obviously, the answers chosen will affect the numbers counted; using a broad definition means that more missing
children will be counted.

A second set of problems concerns reporting. Parents of
missing children presumably call their local law enforcement
agency—usually a police or sheriff's department. But those authorities may respond in different ways. Some states require
them to forward all missing-children reports to a statewide
clearinghouse, which is supposed to contact all law enforcement
agencies in the state in order to facilitate the search. The clear-
inghouses—and some departments—may notify the National

Crime Information Center, a branch of the FBI that compiles missing-persons reports. Some reports also reach the National Center for Missing and Exploited Children (the federally funded group best known for circulating pictures of missing children) or FBI investigators (who claim jurisdiction over a few, but by no means most, kidnappings). Authorities in the same jurisdiction do not necessarily handle all missing-children reports the same way; the case of a six-year-old seen being dragged into a strange car is likely to be treated differently than a report of a sixteen-year-old who has run away. We can suspect that the policies of different agencies will vary significantly. The point is that the jurisdiction from which a child disappears and the particulars of the case probably affect whether a particular missing-child report finds its way into various agencies' records.

It is thus very difficult to make convincing comparisons of the numbers of missing children from either time to time or place to place. Reporters who noted that fewer child-kidnapping reports were filed with the FBI in 2002 than in 2001, and who therefore concluded that the problem was declining, mistakenly assumed that the FBI's records were more complete and authoritative than they actually were. Some things—like missing children—are very difficult to count, which should make us skeptical about the accuracy of statistics that claim to describe the situation.

Such difficulties can create special problems when people try to weigh things that are relatively easy to measure against things that are less calculable. Consider the method of cost-benefit analysis as a basis for decision-making.[8] In principle, it seems straightforward: calculate the expected costs and the value of the expected benefits for different courses of action, and choose the option that promises the best outcome. One problem, however, is that some costs and benefits are easier to compute than others. A teenager trying to decide whether to go to a movie or spend an evening babysitting can probably assign reasonably accurate dollar values to these options—the cost of the movie ticket and refreshments versus the expected earnings from babysitting—but even then the decision will probably hinge on additional assumptions about happiness: would I be happier spending the evening with my friends at a movie, or would I prefer to earn money that can be spent for some greater benefit down the line?

When applied to questions of social policy, such calculations only become more complex. Should we build more highways or support mass transit? Mass transit is rarely self-supporting: if the cost per trip seems too high, riders abandon mass transit; in order to keep them riding, ticket prices usually must be kept low by subsidizing the system. Critics of mass transit sometimes argue that such subsidies are wrong, that mass transit is inefficient, expensive, and therefore not competitive. Advocates respond that this critique ignores many of the relevant costs and benefits. Whereas riders directly bear the costs of using mass transit each time they buy a ticket, the ways we pay for the costs of highway travel are less obvious (for example, through gasoline taxes). Moreover, highways carry hidden, quality of life costs, such as greater air pollution, more traffic fatalities, and cities that discourage foot traffic by devoting huge areas to roads and parking lots. But such costs are hard to calculate. Even if we can agree on the likely health costs from air pollution and traffic accidents, how can we hope to assign a dollar value to being able to comfortably walk from one destination to another? And, of course, the critics have a rebuttal: costs are also incurred in building and maintaining mass transit systems. And what about the freedom cars offer—the ability to choose your own route and schedule? Shouldn't these considerations be incorporated in any calculations?

There are basically two solutions to the problems that intangible factors pose to cost-benefit analyses, but neither solution is completely satisfactory. The first is to leave these factors out of the equation, to simply ignore what seems impossible to quantify. But should factors such as quality of life be treated as irrelevant simply because they are hard to measure? The second solution is to estimate the values of costs and benefits, to assign dollar values to them. This approach keeps these factors in view, but the process is obviously arbitrary—what dollar value should be assigned to comfort or freedom? It is easy to skew the results of any cost-benefit analysis by pegging values as either very high or very low.

Our culture has a particularly difficult time assigning values to certain types of factors. Periodically, for example, the press expresses shock that a cost-benefit analysis has assigned some specific value to individual lives.[9] Such revelations produce predictably outraged challenges: how can anyone place a dollar value on a human life—aren't people's lives priceless? The answer to that question depends on when and where it is asked. Americans' notion that human life is priceless has a surprisingly short history. Only a century ago, the parents of a child killed by a streetcar could sue the streetcar company for damages equal to the child's economic value to the family (basically, the child's expected earnings until adulthood); today, of course, the parents would sue for the (vastly greater) value of their pain and suffering. Even the dollar value of a child's life varies across time and space.[10]

But the larger point is that trade-offs are inevitable. Building a bridge or implementing a childhood vaccination program has both risks and costs—as do the alternatives of not building the bridge or not vaccinating children. Our culture seems to have a lot of difficulty debating whether, say, vaccinations should proceed if they will cause some number of children to sicken and die. Advocates on both sides try to circumvent this debate by creating melodramatically simple alternatives: vaccine proponents can be counted on to declare that harm from vaccines is virtually nonexistent but that failure to vaccinate will have terrible, widespread consequences; whereas opponents predictably insist that vaccines harm many and that they don't do all that much good. Obviously, such debates could use some good data. But, beyond that, we need to recognize that every choice carries costs and that we can weigh and choose only among imperfect options. Even if we can agree that a vaccine will kill a small number of children but will save a great many, how are we to incorporate into our decision-making the notion that every human life is beyond price? How should we weigh the value of a few priceless lives that might be lost if vaccinations proceed against the value of many priceless lives that might be lost if vaccinations are curtailed? (Chapter 3 extends this discussion of trade-offs.)

In short, some numbers are missing from discussions of social issues because certain phenomena are hard to quantify, and any effort to assign numeric values to them is subject to debate. But refusing to somehow incorporate these factors into our calculations creates its own hazards. The best solution is to acknowledge the difficulties we encounter in measuring these phenomena, debate openly, and weigh the options as best we can.

THE UNCOUNTED

A third category of missing numbers involves what is deliberately uncounted, records that go unkept. Consider the U.S. Bureau of the Census's tabulations of religious affiliation: there are none. In fact, the census asks no questions about religion. Arguments about the constitutionally mandated separation of church and state, as well as a general sense that religion is a touchy subject, have led the Census Bureau to omit any questions about religion when it surveys the citizenry (in contrast to most European countries, where such questions are asked).[11]

Thus, anyone trying to estimate the level of religious activity in the United States must rely on less accurate numbers, such as church membership rolls or individuals' reports of their attendance at worship services. The membership rolls of different denominations vary in what they count: Are infants counted once baptized, or does one become an enrolled member only in childhood or even adulthood? Are individuals culled from the rolls if they stop attending or actively participating in religious activities? Such variation makes it difficult to compare the sizes of different faiths (as discussed further in chapter 6). Surveys other than the census sometimes ask people how often they attend religious services, but we have good reason to suspect that respondents overreport attendance (possibly to make a good impression on the interviewers).[12] The result is that, for the United States, at least, it is difficult to accurately measure the population's religious preferences or level of involvement. The policy of not asking questions about religion through the census means that such information simply does not exist.

The way choices are phrased also creates uncounted categories. Since 1790, each census has asked about race or ethnicity, but the wording of the questions—and the array of possible answers—has changed. The 2000 census, for example, was the first to offer respondents the chance to identify themselves as multiracial. Proponents of this change had argued that many Americans have family trees that include ancestors of different races and that it was unreasonable to force people to place themselves within a single racial category.

But some advocates had another reason for promoting this change. When forced to choose only one category, people who knew that their family backgrounds included people of different ethnicities had to oversimplify; most probably picked the option that fit the largest share of their ancestors. For example, an individual whose grandparents included three whites and one Native American was likely to choose "white." In a society in which a group's political influence depends partly on its size, such choices could depress the numbers of people of American Indian ancestry (or any other relatively small, heavily intermarried group) identified by the census. Native American activists favored letting people list themselves as being of more than one race because they believed that this would help identify a larger Native American population and presumably increase that group's political clout. In contrast, African American activists tended to be less enthusiastic about allowing people to identify themselves as multiracial. Based in part on the legacy of segregation, which sometimes held that having a single black ancestor was sufficient to warrant being considered nonwhite, people with mixed black and white ancestry (who account for a majority of those usually classified as African Americans) had tended to list themselves as "black." If large numbers of these individuals began listing more than one racial group, black people might risk losing political influence. As is so often the case, attitudes toward altering the census categories depended on whether one expected to win or lose by the change. The reclassification had the expected effect, even though only 2.4 percent of respondents to the 2000 census opted to describe themselves as multiracial. The new classification boosted the numbers of people classified as Native Americans: although only 2.5 million respondents listed themselves under the traditional one-ethnicity category, adding those who identified themselves as part-Indian raised the total to 4.1 million—a 110 percent increase since 1990. However, relatively small numbers of people (fewer than eight hundred thousand) listed their race as both white and black, compared to almost 34 million identified as black.[13]

Sometimes only certain cases go uncounted. Critics argue that the official unemployment rate, which counts only those without full-time work who have actively looked for a job during the previous four weeks, is too low. They insist that a more accurate count would include those who want to work but have given up looking as well as those who want full-time work but have had to settle for part-time jobs—two groups that, taken together, actually outnumber the officially unemployed.[14] Of course, every definition draws such distinctions between what does—and doesn't—count.

The lesson is simple. Statistics depend on collecting information. If questions go unasked, or if they are asked in ways that limit responses, or if measures count some cases but exclude others, information goes ungathered, and missing numbers result. Nevertheless, choices regarding which data to collect and how to go about collecting the information are inevitable. If we want to describe America's racial composition in a way that can be understood, we need to distill incredible diversity into a few categories. The cost of classifying anything into a particular set of categories is that some information is inevitably lost: distinctions seem sharper; what may have been arbitrary cut-offs are treated as meaningful; and, in particular, we tend to lose sight of the choices and uncertainties that went into creating our categories.

In some cases, critics argue that a failure to gather information is intentional, a method of avoiding the release of damaging information. For example, it has proven very difficult to collect information about the circumstances under which police shoot civilians. We might imagine that police shootings can be divided into two categories: those that are justified by the circumstances, and those that are not. In fact, many police departments conduct reviews of shootings to designate them as justifiable or not. Yet efforts to collect national data on these findings have foundered. Not all departments share their records (which, critics say, implies that they have something to hide); and the proportion of shootings labeled "justified" varies wildly from department to department (suggesting either that police behave very differently in different departments or that the process of reviewing shootings varies a great deal).[15]

There are a variety of ways to ensure that things remain uncounted. The simplest is to not collect the information (for instance, don't ask census respondents any questions about religion). But, even when the data exist, it is possible to avoid compiling information (by simply not doing the calculations necessary to produce certain statistics), to refuse to publish the information, or even to block access to it.[16] More subtly, both data collection and analysis can be time-consuming and expensive; in a society where researchers depend on others for funding, decisions not to fund certain research can have the effect of relegating those topics to the ranks of the uncounted.

This works both ways. Inevitably, we also hear arguments that people *should* stop gathering some sorts of numbers. For example, a popular guide to colleges for prospective students offers a ranking of "party schools." A Matter of Degree—a program sponsored by the American Medical Association to fight alcohol abuse on college campuses—claims that this ranking makes light of and perhaps contributes to campus drinking problems and has called for the guidebook to stop publishing the list.[17] While it is probably uncommon for critics to worry that statistics might be a harmful moral influence, all sorts of data, some will contend, might be better left uncollected—and therefore missing.

THE FORGOTTEN

Another form of missing numbers is easy to overlook—these are figures, once public and even familiar, that we no longer remember or don't bother to consider. Consider the number of deaths from measles. In 1900, the death rate from measles was 13.3 per 100,000 in the population; measles ranked among the top ten diseases causing death in the United States. Over the course of a century, however, measles lost its power to kill; first more effective treatments and then vaccination eliminated measles as a major medical threat. Nor was this an exceptional case. At the beginning of the twentieth century, many of the leading causes of death were infectious diseases; influenza/pneumonia, tuberculosis, diphtheria, and typhoid/typhoid fever also ranked in the top ten.[18] Most of those formerly devastating diseases have been brought under something approaching complete control in the United States through the advent of vaccinations and antibiotics. The array of medical threats has changed.

Forgotten numbers have the potential to help us put things in perspective, if only we can bring ourselves to remember them. When we lose sight of the past, we have more trouble assessing our current situation. However, people who are trying to draw attention to social problems are often reluctant to make comparisons with the past. After all, such comparisons may reveal considerable progress. During the twentieth century, for example, Americans' life expectancies increased dramatically. In 1900, a newborn male could expect to live forty-six years; a century later, male life expectancy had risen to seventy-three. The increase for females was even greater—from age forty-eight to eighty. During the same period, the proportion of Americans completing high school rose from about 6 percent to about 85 percent. Many advocates seem to fear that talking about long-term progress invites complacency about contemporary society, and they prefer to focus on short-run trends—especially if the numbers seem more compelling because they show things getting worse.[19]

Similarly, comparing our society to others can help us get a better sense of the size and shape of our problems. Again, in discussions of social issues, such comparisons tend to be made selectively, in ways that emphasize the magnitude of our contemporary problems. Where data suggest that the United States lags behind other nations, comparative statistics are commonplace, but we might suspect that those trying to promote social action will be less likely to present evidence showing America to advantage. (Of course, those resisting change may favor just such numbers.) Comparisons across time and space are recalled when they help advocates make their points, but otherwise they tend to be ignored, if not forgotten.

LEGENDARY NUMBERS

One final category deserves mention. It does not involve potentially relevant numbers that are missing, but rather includes irrelevant or erroneous figures that somehow find their way into discussions of social issues. Recently, for example, it became fairly common for journalists to compare various risks against a peculiar standard: the number of people killed worldwide each year by falling coconuts (the annual coconut-death figure usually cited was 150). Do 150 people actually die in this way? It might seem possible—coconuts are hard and heavy, and they fall a great distance, so being bonked on the head presumably might be fatal. But who keeps track of coconut fatalities? The answer: no one. Although it turns out that the medical literature includes a few reports of injuries—not deaths—inflicted by falling coconuts, the figure of 150 deaths is the journalistic equivalent of a contemporary legend.[20] It gets passed along as a "true fact," repeated as something that "everybody knows."

Other legendary statistics are attributed to presumably authoritative sources. A claim that a World Health Organization study had determined that blondness was caused by a recessive gene and that blonds would be extinct within two hundred years was carried by a number of prominent news outlets, which presumably ran the story on the basis of one another's coverage, without bothering to check with the World Health Organization (which denied the story).[21]

Legendary numbers can become surprisingly well established. Take the claim that fifty-six is the average age at which a woman becomes widowed. In spite of its obvious improbability (after all, the average male lives into his seventies, married men live longer than those who are unmarried, and husbands are only a few years older on average than their wives), this statistic has circulated for more than twenty years. It appeared in a television commercial for financial services, in materials distributed to women's studies students, and in countless newspaper and magazine articles; its origins are long lost. Perhaps it has endured because no official agency collects data on age at widowhood, making it difficult to challenge such a frequently repeated figure. Nevertheless, demographers—using complicated equations that incorporate age-specific death rates, the percentage of married people in various age cohorts, and age differences between husbands and wives—have concluded that the average age at which women become widows has, to no one's surprise, been rising steadily, from sixty-five in 1970 to about sixty-nine in 1988.[22]

Even figures that actually originate in scientists' statements can take on legendary qualities. In part, this reflects the difficulties of translating complex scientific ideas into what are intended to be easy-to-understand statements. For example, the widely repeated claim that individuals need to drink eight glasses of water each day had its origin in an analysis that did in fact recommend that level of water intake. But the analysis also noted that most of this water would ordinarily come from food (bread, for example, is 35 percent water, and meats and vegetables contain even higher proportions of water). However, the notion that food contained most of the water needed for good health was soon forgotten, in favor of urging people to consume the entire amount through drinking.[23] Similarly, the oft-repeated statements that humans and chimpanzees have DNA that is 98 percent similar—or, variously, 98.4, 99, or 99.44 percent similar—may seem precise, but they ignore the complex assumptions involved in making such calculations and imply that this measure is more meaningful than it actually is.[24]

Widely circulated numbers are not necessarily valid or even meaningful. In the modern world, with ready access to the Internet and all manner of electronic databases, even figures that have been thoroughly debunked can remain in circulation; they are easy to retrieve and disseminate but almost impossible to eradicate. The problem is not one of missing numbers—in such cases, the numbers are all too present. What is absent is the sort of evidence needed to give the statistics any credibility.

The attraction of legendary numbers is that they seem to give weight or authority to a claim. It is far less convincing to argue, "That's not such an important cause of death! Why, I'll bet more people are killed each year by falling coconuts!" than to flatly compare 150 coconut deaths to whatever is at issue. Numbers are presumed to be factual; numbers imply that someone has actually counted something. Of course, if that is true, it should be possible to document the claim—which cannot be done for legendary numbers.

A related phenomenon is that some numbers, if not themselves fanciful, come to be considered more meaningful than they are. (Chapter 5 also addresses this theme.) We see this particularly in the efforts of bureaucrats to measure the unmeasurable. A school district, for example, might want to reward good teaching. But what makes a good teacher? Most of us can look back on our teachers and identify some as better than others. But what made them better? Maybe they helped us when we were having trouble, encouraged us, or set high standards. My reasons for singling out some of my teachers as especially good might be very different from the reasons you would cite. Teachers can be excellent in many ways, and there's probably no reliable method of translating degree of excellence into a number. How can we measure good teaching or artistic genius? Even baseball fans—those compulsive recordkeepers and lovers of statistics—can argue about the relative merits of different athletes, and baseball has remarkably complete records of players' performances.

But that sort of soft appeal to the immeasurability of performance is unlikely to appease politicians or an angry public demanding better schools. So educational bureaucrats—school districts and state education departments—insist on measuring "performance." In recent years, the favored measure has been students' scores on standardized tests. This is not completely unreasonable—one could argue that, overall, better teaching should lead to students learning more and, in turn, to higher test scores. But test scores are affected by many things besides teachers' performance, including students' home lives. And our own memories of our "best teachers" probably don't depend on how they shaped our performances on standardized tests.

However imperfect test scores might be as an indicator of the quality of teaching, they do offer a nice quantitative measure— this student got so many right, the students in this class scored this well, and so on. No wonder bureaucrats gravitate toward such measures—they are precise (and it is relatively inexpensive to get the information), even if it isn't clear just what they mean. The same thing happens in many settings. Universities want their professors to do high-quality research and be good teachers, but everyone recognizes that these qualities are hard to measure. Thus, there is a tremendous temptation to focus on things that are easy to count: How many books or articles has a faculty member published? (Some departments even selectively weigh articles in different journals, depending on some measure of each journal's influence.) Are a professor's teaching evaluation scores better than average?

The problem with such bureaucratic measures is that we lose sight of their limitations. We begin by telling ourselves that we need some way of measuring teaching quality and that this method—whatever its flaws—is better than nothing. Even if some resist adopting the measure at first, over time inertia sets in, and people come to accept its use. Before long, the measure is taken for granted, and its flaws tend to be forgotten. The criticism of being an imperfect measure can be leveled at many of the numbers discussed in the chapters that follow. If pressed, a statistic's defenders will often acknowledge that the criticism is valid, that the measure is flawed. But, they ask, what choice do we have? How else can we measure—quickly, cheaply, and more or less objectively—good teaching (or whatever else concerns us)? Isn't an imperfect statistic better than none at all? They have a point. But we should never blind ourselves to a statistic's shortcomings; once we forget a number's limitations, we give it far more power and influence than it deserves. We need to remember that a clear and direct measure would be preferable and that our imperfect measure is—once again—a type of missing number.

WHAT'S MISSING?

When people use statistics, they assume—or, at least, they want their listeners to assume—that the numbers are meaningful. This means, at a minimum, that someone has actually counted something and that they have done the counting in a way that makes sense. Statistical information is one of the best ways we have of making sense of the world's complexities, of identifying patterns amid the confusion. But bad statistics give us bad information.

This chapter argues that some statistics are bad not so much because the information they contain is bad but because of what is missing—what has not been counted. Numbers can be missing in several senses: a powerful example can make us forget to look for statistics; things can go uncounted because they are considered difficult or impossible to count or because we decide not to count them. In other cases, we count, but something gets lost in the process: things once counted are forgotten, or we brandish numbers that lack substance.

In all of these cases, something is missing. Understanding that helps us recognize what counts as a good statistic. Good statistics are not only products of people counting; the quality of statistics also depends on people's willingness and ability to count thoughtfully and on their decisions about what, exactly, ought to be counted so that the resulting numbers will be both accurate and meaningful.

This process is never perfect. Every number has its limitations; every number is a product of choices that inevitably involve compromise. Statistics are intended to help us summarize, to get an overview of part of the world's complexity. But some information is always sacrificed in the process of choosing what will be counted and how. Something is, in short, always missing. In evaluating statistics, we should not forget what has been lost, if only because this helps us understand what we still have.

A recent newspaper column by a prominent political commentator began: "It is a truism in politics that around 40 percent of Republicans will always vote for a Republican presidential candidate and about the same percentage of Democrats will vote for their party's candidate. The battle is for the middle 20 percent."[1] Percentages–1; pundit–0. Numbers that appear to be simple can confuse even people who are paid to provide insight to the rest of us. And there is no shortage of confusing numbers.

For instance, claims made in the debate over the proposed 2003 federal tax cut seemed contradictory. The bill's proponents declared that the average family's tax reduction would be more than $1,000, but the bill's opponents noted that more than half of all families would have their taxes cut by less than $100.[2] In other words, the average benefit would be either a lot (according to those favoring the bill) or a little (according to the opposition). Confused?

Most of us assume that we understand what *average* means. Although many critics bemoan our innumeracy—our discomfort with numbers—Americans actually consume a steady diet of familiar statistics that involve averages, percentages, and the like.[3] Crime rates, stock market indexes, and batting averages are the stuff not only of daily news reports but of routine, everyday conversations. The assumption is that we grasp these numbers—and we probably do, more or less.

However, familiarity can breed confusion. Even apparently simple, straightforward numbers can pose traps for the unwary. Inappropriate statistics may be offered, or appropriate numbers may be used in inappropriate ways. The result is confusion. Perhaps we know we're confused (we realize that we don't understand the figures), or perhaps we don't (we imagine that we understand numbers when we actually do not). Sometimes the people who give us a bad number may themselves be confused; in other cases, they know what they're doing, and they're trying to hoodwink us.

There are many routes to statistical confusion, and this chapter cannot hope to discuss more than a few. While understanding some of the most frequently encountered problems will require coming to grips with a few basic mathematical and logical principles, our real concern will be exploring how social processes—that is, people counting—contribute to these errors. The chapter begins with common problems that involve familiar statistics, such as averages and percentages, and then addresses special issues raised by confusing graphs.

The simplest statistic is, of course, a count—someone tallies up a total and reports it: our town has so many residents, its police force recorded this many crime reports last year, and so on. Counts can be flawed, particularly when the items being counted are partially hidden (which makes it difficult to get a complete count) or when they are very common (which can make counting so expensive that we must settle for cheaper but less accurate estimates). There is also the issue of what counts—it is important to understand how what is being counted is defined and measured.[4] But, overall, a count seems remarkably straightforward. The concept is easy to understand; we've all counted things. A count is a single number that corresponds clearly to a familiar notion: how many are there? It is difficult to get confused about a count. Alas, the same cannot be said for other simple statistics; even basic arithmetic can inspire confusion.

Averages

One of the most common sorts of arithmetic confusion involves the concept of an average. The standard method of calculating an average, learned in some half-forgotten arithmetic class and usually taken for granted, is to total up scores and divide by the number of cases. If a group of children take a 10-word spelling test, we can add the number of words each child spelled correctly and divide that total by the number of children to give us the group's average score—say, 8.2 words spelled correctly.

The average calculated using this familiar method is technically termed the *mean*. The mean is a useful measure as long as the scores do not vary wildly. (A child's score on our spelling test cannot be lower than 0 or higher than 10, for instance.) But imagine a factory with ninety workers, each earning $40,000; nine managers, each earning $80,000; and a chief executive officer, who brings home—I am somehow hesitant to write "earns"—say, $6 million. We calculate the mean income for the people working in our factory as follows:

90 × $ 40,000 =	$ 3,600,000	income total for workers
9 × $ 80,000 =	$ 720,000	income total for managers
1 × $ 6,000,000 =	$ 6,000,000	income total for the CEO

	$ 10,320,000	(total income)/100 (total people)
=	$ 103,200	mean income

This mean is pretty much meaningless. No one at the factory earns the average; the nine managers' salaries ($80,000) are closest to the mean, but that average figure ($103,200) is far removed from either the workers' earnings or the CEO's income.

One solution to this problem is to present a different measure of the average—the median, instead of the mean. The *median* is the middle case in a distribution. To calculate the median, we list the cases in the order of their scores, from the lowest to the highest, and then take the value of the middle score. In our factory example, with one hundred people, the fiftieth and fifty-first lowest incomes are in the middle. Both of these incomes are $40,000, so the median income for our factory is $40,000. In this case, the median score gives a more accurate sense of a typical income than the mean—after all, 90 percent of the people in our factory earn $40,000, making it the typical salary. Because income distributions often include figures that vary wildly, the median is the preferred measure, used to give a better sense of what is average. Thus, we regularly encounter references to the "median household income" and so on.

Whether we choose the mean or the median to express what is average, we lose some information. In our factory example, 99 percent of the people earned less than the mean income, so $103,200 is an average only in a very peculiar sense. But using the $40,000 median forces us to lose sight of those people who make more—in the CEO's case, vastly more. The median is probably the preferable figure in this case, but neither measure is perfect; no single number clearly conveys exactly how our imaginary factory distributes income. And which figure you prefer may depend on the point you want to make: using the mean might help to emphasize the substantial income generated by the factory, while using the median serves to highlight the workers' modest incomes. It is not difficult to find examples of such differences: in those contradictory tax-cut claims at the beginning of this chapter, notice how the bill's proponents referred to the mean tax reduction as average, whereas opponents pointed to the median figure. Whenever we confront an average, we should be able to tell whether it has been calculated as a mean or a median. Ideally, we might also consider whether knowing the other figure might change our impression of what's average.

Percentages

The percentage is probably our handiest statistic: simple to calculate, incredibly useful, yet almost intuitively easy to understand. In its simplest form—when dividing a whole into parts—it presents few problems. If we are told that about 10 percent of people write with their left hand, then we can calculate that roughly 90 percent use their right hand to write, that there are about nine right-handed writers for every lefty, and so on.

However, because the percentage is such a familiar and useful tool, it often is used to present somewhat more complicated sorts of information. And things don't have to get much more complicated before we can become confused. Imagine that we do a study of 1,000 adolescents, classifying them as either delinquent or law-abiding, and as either right- or left-handed. Suppose that we find 810 law-abiding righties, 90 delinquent righties, 80 law-abiding lefties, and 20 delinquent lefties. (Before someone gets offended, let me emphasize that these are imaginary data, meant only to illustrate a point.) To help sort through those numbers and make sense of them, let's arrange our data as shown in Table 1, with cells for each of the four possible combinations of handedness and delinquency.

Table 1. *Raw Numbers (fairly confusing)*

	Right-Handed	Left-Handed
Law-abiding	810	80
Delinquent	90	20

That didn't help all that much, did it? Let's see what happens in Table 2, in which we calculate percentages across the table so that each row totals 100 percent. (Note that here and in the following tables I've included the number of people in parentheses in each cell, along with the percentages, which allows you to check my calculations.) Table 2 clearly conveys the idea that right-handers account for substantial majorities of both law-abiding and delinquent adolescents. But that's not terribly interesting, since we already know that right-handers outnumber left-handers.

Table 2. *Calculating Percentages Across (still confusing)*

	Right-Handed	Left-Handed	Total
Law-abiding	91% (810)	9% (80)	100% (890)
Delinquent	82% (90)	18% (20)	100% (110)

But watch what happens when we calculate the percentages down, as shown in Table 3, so that each column totals 100 percent. Suddenly, the pattern becomes clear: in our study, the percentage of lefties who are delinquent (20 percent) is twice that of righties (10 percent). These percentages help us understand the pattern in the numbers.

Table 3. *Calculating Percentages Down (much clearer)*

	Right-Handed	Left-Handed
Law-abiding	90% (810)	80% (80)
Delinquent	10% (90)	20% (20)
Total	100% (900)	100% (100)

Table 2 illustrates what we mean when we say that someone has calculated the percentages "in the wrong direction" or "in the wrong way." In general, percentages should be calculated so that each value of the independent variable (the cause) totals 100 percent. In our example, handedness is obviously the independent variable—no one imagines that being law-abiding or delinquent can cause you to become right- or left-handed, but it is at least conceivable that handedness might somehow affect delinquency.[5] Thus, we need to calculate our percentages so that the columns for right- and left-handed adolescents each add up to 100 percent (as they do in Table 3).

Deciding which way to calculate percentages requires a little thought. Surprisingly often, you can spot people who ought to know better presenting percentages that have been calculated the wrong way. Sometimes, wrong-way percentages can seem impressive. Suppose that someone announces, for instance, that a large percentage of alcoholics—say, 60 percent—experienced abuse as children. (Once more, I am simply inventing numbers for purposes of illustration.) Both the people who make this claim and the people who hear it might consider it to be strong evidence that childhood abuse affects the chances that people will become alcoholics. But alas, this statistic actually gives us the percentages calculated the wrong way.

Let's think this through. One's alcoholism as an adult cannot possibly cause one to have been abused during childhood; therefore, abuse—not alcoholism—must be treated as the cause, the independent variable. What we want to compare is the percentage of people who were abused as children and went on to become alcoholics with the percentage of people who were not abused as children and became alcoholics. That is, we should calculate the percentages for those abused and those not abused so that each totals 100 percent. If the first figure is greater than the second—as it is in Table 4—the data indeed suggest that a history of abuse might affect one's chances of becoming alcoholic.

Table 4. *Imaginary Data Showing That Childhood Abuse Makes Adult Alcoholism More Likely*

	Abused	Not Abused
Alcoholic	20% (120)	10% (80)
Not alcoholic	80% (480)	90% (720)
Total	100% (600)	100% (800)

When we hear that most alcoholics experienced abuse as children, we tend to assume that people who were abused are more likely to become alcoholics, which is what Table 4 shows. In this table, the percentage of alcoholics among those abused as children (20 percent) is twice as great as the percentage of alcoholics among people who were not abused (10 percent). (Note, too, that my imaginary numbers include 200 alcoholics and that 60 percent of them—120 cases—were abused. Thus, these data do support our original statement that 60 percent of alcoholics experienced abuse.)

But now consider Tables 5 and 6, which use different sets of numbers. In Table 5, we see that equal percentages of those abused as children and those who were not abused become alcoholics (20 percent in both instances). These data suggest that childhood abuse has no effect on adult alcoholism. And Table 6 actually shows that people who were not abused as children are more likely to become alcoholics (30 percent) than those who were abused (20 percent).

Table 5. *Imaginary Data Showing That Childhood Abuse Has No Effect on Adult Alcoholism*

	Abused	Not Abused
Alcoholic	20% (120)	20% (80)
Not alcoholic	80% (480)	80% (320)
Total	100% (600)	100% (400)

Table 6. *Imaginary Data Showing That Childhood Abuse Makes Adult Alcoholism Less Likely*

	Abused	Not Abused
Alcoholic	20% (120)	30% (80)
Not alcoholic	80% (480)	70% (189)
Total	100% (600)	100% (269)

Despite these notable differences, a close inspection of the top rows of Tables 4–6 reveals that, in each case, our original wrong-way percentage (60 percent of alcoholics—120 of 200—were abused as children) remains the same. Although presenting percentages calculated in the wrong direction encourages us to imagine that the overall pattern might be the one depicted in Table 4, it is important to understand that all three tables, despite contradictory data, are consistent with that wrong-way percentage. This is precisely what's wrong with calculating percentages the wrong way. Such percentages confuse rather than clarify.

Confusion can also result when we use percentages to describe a sequence of changes. Suppose we learn that a stock index fell 50 percent between 1980 and 1990 but then rose 95 percent between 1990 and 2000. Was the value in 2000 greater than in 1980? At first glance, it might seem so ("down 50 percent, but then back up 95 percent, and 95 is way more than 50 . . ."), but the answer is no.

Assume that the index's 1980 value was 1,000. A 50 percent decline by 1990 would cause the value to fall to 500 (50 percent of 1,000 is 500, which we subtract from the original 1,000). The 95 percent rise between 1990 and 2000, however, must be measured against the 1990 value (95 percent of 500 is 475, which we add to the 1990 value of 500, for a total of 975—which is less than the 1980 figure of 1,000). That is, a percentage change is always calculated against the figure at the beginning of the change. In describing any series of changes (such as the shifts from 1980 to 1990 to 2000), the outcome of one change creates a new basis from which the next change is calculated. Thus while each single change may seem easy to understand, we need to think carefully when we start comparing a series of percentage changes.

Quick, try this calculation: if our total stock index rose 50 percent between 1980 and 1990 and then fell 95 percent between 1990 and 2000, which value is greater—the one for 1980 or the one for 2000? The answer, of course, is again 1980—and now by a huge margin. Again assume that the 1980 value was 1,000. A 50 percent increase would cause a rise to 1,500 in 1990, but a 95 percent fall from 1,500 would produce a figure of only 75 for the year 2000. The lesson is simple: a series of changes expressed in percentages creates numbers that aren't really comparable.[6] People who present information in this way are probably either themselves confused or trying to pull a fast one.

Although the ideas of averages and percentages are familiar

and seemingly straightforward, they retain the potential to confuse us. So it should be no surprise that confusion arises even more easily as statistical ideas become more complex.

The Meaning of Correlation

One of the most important forms of reasoning occurs when we recognize that two things are related ("when I flip this switch up, the light goes on; and when I flip it down, the light goes off"). This recognition invites us to suspect that one thing may cause the other, which lets us better understand our world and plan our actions based on what we think we know ("it's too dark, so I'll try flipping the switch").

Patterned relationships between two things can take many forms: every time A goes up, B goes up; every time A goes up, B goes down; when A goes up, B is slightly more likely to go up; and so on. Philosophers and scientists classify these relationships as forms of *correlation*. When we say that A and B are correlated, we are noting some sort of observable relationship between them, whether it is a perfect one-to-one correspondence (the light goes on every time the switch is flipped up, and only when the switch goes up) or only a slight tendency (people who were abused as children are somewhat more likely to become alcoholics).

Such relationships may be causal. We understand, for example, that flipping the switch causes the light to go on. But that understanding is grounded on more than observation; we also have a theory to explain the relationship (flipping the switch closes a circuit that allows electrical current to flow through the lightbulb, heating the filament until it gives off light). Our theory could be wrong, but in this case we know that lots of people have tested the theory of electricity, and it predicts so well that we have great confidence in it.

But—and this is the key point—while causality cannot exist without correlation, correlation is not itself sufficient to prove causality. Just because two things seem related does not mean that one causes the other. To return to our imaginary research about childhood abuse and alcoholism, suppose that we do find that people who were abused as children are more likely to become alcoholics than people who were not abused (in other words, imagine that we have evidence of the sort shown in Table 4). Such findings do not constitute proof that childhood abuse causes adult alcoholism. It is possible that the abuse-alcoholism relationship is *spurious*—that is, some third variable might cause the variation in both abuse and alcoholism. For example, perhaps it is the case that poor families have higher rates of child abuse and that people raised in poverty are more likely to become alcoholics. If we expand the data in Table 4 by also asking whether the people in our study were raised in poor families, we might get the (imaginary) results shown in Table 7.

Table 7. *Imaginary Data Showing That Childhood Poverty, Not Childhood Abuse, Makes Adult Alcoholism More Likely*

	Raised Poor		Not Raised Poor	
	Abused	Not Abused	Abused	Not Abused
Alcoholic	25% (112)	25% (50)	5% (8)	5% (30)
Not alcoholic	75% (330)	75% (150)	95% (152)	95% (570)
Total	100% (442)	100% (200)	100% (160)	100% (600)

Suddenly, what looked like a strong relationship between abuse and alcoholism disappears. In Table 7, we see that childhood abuse has no effect on adult alcoholism, once we take childhood poverty into account. This method of analysis is called controlling for a third variable, which in this case is childhood poverty. The relationship between abuse and alcoholism now seems spurious because the correlation between the two variables is in fact explained by a third variable (poverty). Again, my point in presenting these imaginary numbers is not to endorse some argument about the actual relationship between poverty, childhood abuse, and alcoholism.[7] Rather, I simply want to demonstrate that, even when we calculate our percentages in the right direction, an apparent relationship between two variables can vanish into spuriousness.

In contrast, a genuinely causal relationship is not spurious. But this raises a huge logical problem: we can never prove absolutely that a relationship is not spurious, because it is always possible that some unexamined variable, if only we considered it, would expose the relationship as spurious. Thus, one can always protest that causality cannot be absolutely proven. This argument was the defense adopted by the tobacco industry when, for decades, it insisted that research showing a relationship between smoking and lung cancer did not prove that smoking caused cancer. Strictly speaking, they were right. Of course, by the same logic, we cannot know absolutely that flipping the light switch causes the light to shine.

Any claim that we have identified a causal relationship must be examined critically. I have already suggested several ways of testing such claims. We can *demand some sort of theory,* that is, an argument about the causal process that connects the two variables (electrical current flows through a closed circuit; tobacco smoke irritates lung tissues). We can *identify likely third variables and check* to see whether they are sources of spuriousness. In addition, we can *compile evidence* by doing more studies. Although any piece of research has limitations, if we compile many studies—each with somewhat different limitations—whose results support one another, we begin to have greater confidence in our findings. This is why the evidence for the link between smoking and lung cancer now seems overwhelming. A vast research literature exists, based on many different methods—everything from tracing the smoking histories of people with lung cancer to comparing the proportion of lung cancer deaths among smokers and nonsmokers to inducing lung cancer in laboratory animals by exposing them to smoke, and so on. While each method has its own limitations, studies using all of these methods produce results that support the smoking–lung cancer link, offering strong evidence for a causal relationship.

A related problem occurs when people attribute causality after the fact. In such cases, we spot a relationship, and because one variable logically precedes the other, we assume that it must be the cause. This train of thought combines elements of correct and fallacious reasoning. The correct reasoning is that a cause must occur before its effect; if we can prove that B occurs after A, then we know that B cannot cause A. The fallacy is that A is not necessarily the cause simply because A precedes B—remember that the relationship between A and B may be spurious.

Most heroin addicts report having smoked marijuana at some point before they began using heroin. But can we assume that marijuana use in some way causes heroin use? On the one hand, the fact that marijuana smoking usually precedes trying heroin is not proof of causality—after all, just about every addict also ate ice cream at some point before using heroin, and we don't peg ice cream as a cause of addiction. But that critique is obviously imperfect: marijuana, unlike ice cream, is illegal; and we might reasonably suspect that dabbling in one illegal drug might foster more serious drug use. On the other hand, the relationship between marijuana smoking and heroin use is very weak: only a small fraction of those who try marijuana become heroin addicts.

Some contemporary critics of drug use try to gloss over the issue of causality by declaring that marijuana is a "gateway" drug—that is, marijuana use may not cause heroin addiction, but it might be a gateway through which most heroin users pass on their way to addiction.[8] This analogy, however, is ambiguous; it does not specify the nature of the link between marijuana and heroin. After all, what is a gateway? Should we envision a gate that we could somehow keep closed? In other words, if we could keep people from trying marijuana, could we ensure that they would not try heroin? Or is the gateway just a well-trodden path among a set of alternative routes, so that closing the gate wouldn't have much effect? And what should we think about those marijuana smokers who do not become addicts? To be sure, most heroin addicts have passed through the marijuana gateway, but relatively few of the people who go through that gateway go on to become addicts. The gateway notion is too vague to be much help in understanding drug problems or weighing policy options. Thinking about causality needs to be less sloppy.

These issues barely begin to consider the complexities of correlations between variables. The formal study of statistics—the content of most chapters in most statistics textbooks—is devoted largely to this topic, to measures of the strength of relationships between variables. (In those textbooks, the term *correlation* also has a narrower, technical meaning, as a particular way of thinking about and measuring such relationships.) Such sophisticated calculations have become far more common, thanks to the widespread availability of powerful computers and easily mastered statistical software packages. Statistical procedures that, thirty years ago, required using one of the large mainframe computers available only at a few universities now can be completed on a typical student's standard desktop computer. Today, virtually anyone can produce—if not necessarily understand—highly sophisticated statistics. This ability has created a continual escalation in the complexity of statistical analyses, in an effort to specify increasingly complicated relationships among ever more variables, by using measures that ever fewer people can hope to understand.

Nonetheless, the basic principles regarding correlations between variables are not that difficult to understand. We must look for patterns that reveal potential relationships and for evidence that variables are actually related. But when we do spot those relationships, we should not jump to conclusions about causality. Instead, we need to weigh the strength of the relationship and the plausibility of our theory, and we must always try to discount the possibility of spuriousness.

GETTING CONFUSED WITH GRAPHS

As we've seen, words—and numbers—can indeed be confusing. Perhaps it's time to turn to an approach that seems more

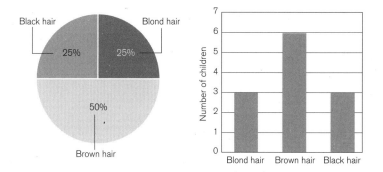

FIGURE 1. A simple pie chart *(left)* and bar graph *(right)* representing the hair color of an imaginary group of children.

basic and more easily understood. We sometimes use the word *envision* to refer to our ability to comprehend information. So let's see whether we can't transform statistics into clearer, visual displays.

Graphs such as simple pie charts, bar graphs, and line graphs are among the most familiar methods of conveying statistical patterns. The basic idea is to represent numbers as pictures. The essential standard for judging graphs is remarkably simple: an accurate display should present visual proportions equivalent to the numeric proportions being represented. To take a very straightforward example, suppose that we have a group of twelve children in which three have blond hair, six have brown hair, and three have black hair. We could convey this information in a pie chart or in a bar graph, as shown in Figure 1.

In both graphs, numbers are translated into spatial equivalents. Half of the children have brown hair, so their slice of the pie chart is equal to half; similarly, because twice as many children have brown hair as have either blond or black hair, the bar for brown hair is twice as tall as the other two bars. In both representations, visual proportions reflect numeric proportions.

The Damaging Effects of Aesthetics

Graphs seem so obvious and intuitive that you might think it would be difficult to louse them up. In fact, it is surprisingly easy, and it has become easier in recent years. In large part, bad graphs are driven by aesthetics. People want their graphs to seem striking, attention-getting. The graphs in Figure 2, for example, are boring because they don't display dramatic differences. In contrast, those in Figure 3, which present exactly the same information, seem interesting.

The two sets of graphs differ only in their vertical scales. Both graphs in the first pair (Figure 2) are drawn to show the full range of possible values, beginning with zero at the bottom and ranging up to a value a bit above the highest number being graphed. These graphs have the virtue of keeping visual proportions true to numeric proportions. The problem, of course, is that they are hard to read—it is difficult to see much difference among the bar graph's bars or much fluctuation in the line on the line graph.

Of course, we almost always want to use graphs to display differences or change; it is usually the differences—not the similarities—that tell the story. While in theory the least deceptive graph is one with a full vertical scale (as in Figure 2), that scale can obscure the differences. One popular solution is to truncate the graph, that is, to cut off the bottom portion of the vertical scale, producing graphs such as those in Figure 3. This ap-

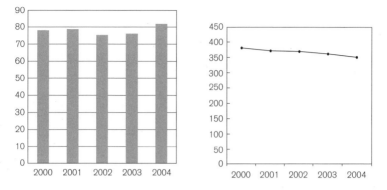

FIGURE 2. A bar graph *(left)* and a line graph *(right)* with zero as the base minimize differences.

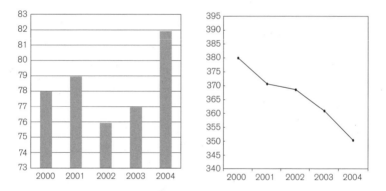

FIGURE 3. A bar graph *(left)* and a line graph *(right)* whose bases have been selected to emphasize differences.

proach is not necessarily illegitimate, as long as you carefully label the values so that readers can understand that the graph has been truncated. Truncating the scale has the effect of making the graph more visually interesting; by emphasizing differences and changes, it highlights the data's dramatic qualities.

Some authorities argue that it is never acceptable to truncate bar graphs (because the relative heights of the bars usually convey the key information), but that it may make sense to truncate line graphs (with clear labeling) where the focus is the pattern of changes. Many newspapers, for example, publish daily line graphs that display the previous day's stock market fluctuations; these graphs are truncated and change their vertical scales from day to day, to emphasize shifts during the previous day's activity. While their different scales mean that the graph published on one day cannot be compared to that published on the next, the papers' readers presumably understand these limitations.

Several relatively recent changes have magnified the disruptive influence of aesthetics in the creation of graphs. One of the most important is the widespread availability of graphics-producing software. Today, pie charts are everywhere, although the old-fashioned method of drawing them by hand with a compass, ruler, and protractor is becoming a lost art. Instead, creating pie charts with a computer has become so simple that people don't give it a thought—and it shows.

Consider Figure 4. This pie chart accompanied a newspaper story about children who had been abducted by family members; it shows the various durations of the abductions.

The chart is confusing for two reasons. First, the slices of the pie are not arranged in any clear order. If we move clockwise around the pie, we read: "One week to less than a month," "One month to less than six months," "One to six hours," "Twenty-four hours to less than a week," and "Other." The sequence makes no sense; the chart confuses more than it clarifies.

Second, the chart contains that peculiar "Other" category.

Duration of abduction

FIGURE 4. A confusing pie chart depicting the duration of child abductions by family members. (*Source:* Ryan Cormier, "A Missing Child, Unbearable Pain," *The News Journal,* Wilmington, DE, July 13, 2003, p. A9; used by permission.)

What does it include? This chart was based on a table published in a government report.[9] Examining the original table reveals that the 22 percent listed as "Other" in the chart includes the following:

Abductions lasting less than one hour	3 percent
Abductions lasting seven to twenty-four hours	4 percent
Abductions lasting more than six months	6 percent
Children not returned but located	6 percent
Cases for which there is no information	3 percent
Total	22 percent

Presumably, the chartmaker grouped these categories together because they were all relatively small, but the result is incoherent: the "Other" category includes some very brief episodes, some very long ones, and some about which, apparently, noth-

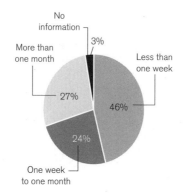

No information
3%
More than one month
Less than one week
27%
46%
24%
One week to one month

FIGURE 5. An improved pie chart depicting the duration of child abductions by family members.

ing is known. It makes no sense to lump these cases together in a single category.

Different, and more useful, pie charts could be derived from the same data. Figure 5, for example, offers a chart that presents the categories in logical order (from brief to lengthy), does not jumble together very different cases in the same category, and conveys a clear pattern—that abductions of children by family members tend to be brief.

Another problem is that most graphics software packages offer a variety of "attractive" display options—for example, you can tilt a pie chart to view it from an angle instead of head-on, which turns the circular pie into an oval. This may be an aesthetic improvement, but it absolutely undercuts the accuracy and usefulness of the chart, because wedges formed by the equal angles from the center of an oval need not have equal areas. Thus, this method of making a pie chart more interesting and attractive actually violates the central principle of statistical graphics—proportionality of space and numbers—and conveys a distorted, inaccurate impression. Other "improvements" have similarly damaging effects, such as showing the edge of a tilted pie chart to the viewer (so that it seems to be a three-dimensional disk), which exaggerates the visual importance of those slices that can be viewed edge-on.

Similarly, most graphics software packages automatically truncate the vertical scales on bar and line graphs to generate dramatic displays that highlight the differences in the data. For example, I had no difficulty producing the graphs in Figure 3; I entered some imaginary data into a popular spreadsheet program, asked for a bar graph and a line graph, and each one popped up on my computer screen. In sharp contrast, it took a lot more work to produce the full-scale graphs shown in Figure 2, even though they involved exactly the same numbers, because I had to circumvent the software's default option and enter additional commands. (I am ashamed to admit that I could not figure out how to do this; I needed someone familiar with the program to explain the sequence of secret commands.) In short, graphics software often makes it simpler to draw distorted graphs than to draw proportional ones. As is so often the case in life, one major attraction of doing things the wrong way is that it is so much easier.

Computer software that generates statistical graphics is thus a mixed blessing, providing ease of use but almost inviting abuse. Because the software offers default formats, it doesn't take much thought—or care—to produce a graph. As a result, we are bombarded with unnecessary graphs. A full-fledged picture may be worth a thousand words, but the information contained in the typical pie chart can usually be conveyed in a sentence. And the elaborate menus of bells and whistles offered by many software packages, such as tilting a pie chart to expose its edge, or turning a graph's bars into three-dimensional figures and converting the graph's bottom into a slope, intended to add drama, often distort the visual proportions so that the whole purpose of the graph—to help people visualize the relative proportions in the data being presented—is undermined.

A related phenomenon has been journalists' adoption of pictorial elements to "liven up" graphs. Thus, instead of circles divided into wedges or simple bars of different heights, graphs drawn in this style present odd-shaped figures. Take a look at the example shown in Figure 6. The national newspaper *USA Today* helped to popularize this style of graphics, but it is widely used. The problem is that, however pleasing to the eye such illustrations may be, they do a terrible job of conveying information. It is often hard to figure out which spatial elements in the figure correspond to the numbers they are supposed to represent. One of the leading theorists of graphs, Edward J. Tufte, has coined the memorable term *chartjunk* to refer to all of the extraneous elements that convey no information and yet litter many contemporary charts and graphs.[10] In extreme cases, chartjunk can make it next to impossible to decipher the meaning of a graph.

Figure 6 is fairly typical of the little feature graphics that appear in the lower corners of newspaper pages. This one reports the results of an online poll of "self-selected respondents" who were apparently asked, "How much will you or do you owe in student loans?" Unfortunately, the results of any online survey are almost certainly meaningless because the sample is not representative. Not everyone has access to the Internet, only a tiny fraction of those who do are likely to stumble across any par-

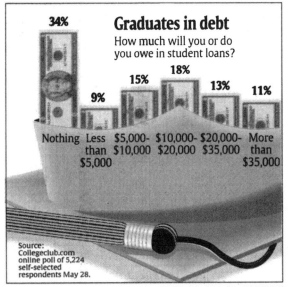

FIGURE 6. The meaning of this graphic is obscured by chartjunk. (*Source: USA Today,* August 6, 2002, p. 1A; © USA Today, reprinted by permission.)

ticular survey, and only some people (which ones? who knows?) will bother completing it. We don't know whether the sample accurately represents the population in question (which, in this case, may be all college students or former students, although we have no way of confirming that either guess is correct). These data, in short, are worthless.

And that's the good news. The graph in Figure 6 contains bars, represented by stylized greenbacks; the bills seem to be sticking out from a graduation cap. (I confess that I puzzled over this drawing for quite a while before I figured out what this was supposed to represent. I was confused by the thing that looks like a pencil with an electrical cord, until I realized that it was intended to be the tassel for the mortarboard.) But there is no way of telling where the bars in the graph begin—somewhere inside that cap, but where? We can tell that 18 percent is greater than 13 percent, which is in turn greater than 11 percent—but then we already knew that. What we don't get is any clear, visual sense of the relative proportions of these quantities, because some unknown part of each bar is hidden from us, and the uneven, peaked contours of the cap suggest that the obscured proportion probably differs from bar to bar.

Making things even more confusing, the viewer's eye is drawn to several features on the cap that might—but on inspection prove not to—represent the baseline for the bars. In addition to the edge of the cap, we have a curved shadow, the cord and tassel, the edge of the mortarboard, and the mortarboard's shadow. This is real chartjunk: it makes the viewer work to decipher meaning from the drawing's features, efforts that will be unrewarded because those features aren't related to any information the graph is supposed to convey. In short, this graph presents meaningless data in an unreadable form—a problem that's increasingly common. Almost any day's newspaper offers examples no better and often much worse, with irregularly shaped pie charts, bar graphs with bars of indeterminate dimensions, and so on.

The combination of aesthetic considerations and computer-assisted graphics can make even straightforward, impeccably labeled graphs prepared by professionals unintentionally deceptive. Consider Figure 7, which reprints bar graphs that first appeared in a publication of the American Sociological Association.

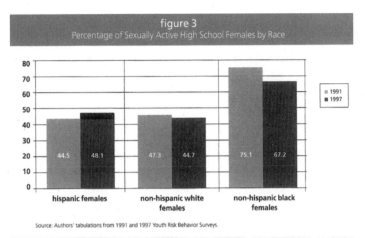

figure 3
Percentage of Sexually Active High School Females by Race

| | 1991 |
| | 1997 |

hispanic females: 44.5, 48.1
non-hispanic white females: 47.3, 44.7
non-hispanic black females: 75.1, 67.2

Source: Authors' tabulations from 1991 and 1997 Youth Risk Behavior Surveys.

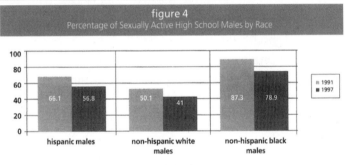

figure 4
Percentage of Sexually Active High School Males by Race

| | 1991 |
| | 1997 |

hispanic males: 66.1, 56.8
non-hispanic white males: 50.1, 41
non-hispanic black males: 87.3, 78.9

Source: Authors' tabulations from 1991 and 1997 Youth Risk Behavior Surveys.

FIGURE 7. A graphic double standard. (*Source:* Barbara Risman and Pepper Schwartz, "After the Sexual Revolution," *Contexts* 1, no. 1 [February 2002]: 19, © 2002 by American Sociological Association; reprinted by permission.)

In reprinting these bar graphs, I have retained the relative proportions found in the original article. The upper graph shows how the percentages of high school females who were sexually active changed between 1991 and 1997, with the data broken down for three ethnic groups (Hispanics, whites, and blacks).

The lower set shows the comparable information for males. Each graph, by itself, is clear. But when they are viewed together, the appearance is deceptive. The page layout allots about half again as much height for the female graph as for the male graph, which consequently has shorter bars. Based on the heights of the bars, our eye tells us that males must have been less sexually active than females, even though a close reading of the percentages reveals that, in five of the six comparisons, males were actually more—sometimes markedly more—sexually active. The effect, probably a result of negligence in laying out the page, is to give a visual impression exactly the opposite of what the data show.

And this is a mild example. It is easy to find pictorial displays of numeric information that are almost impossible to decipher, in which considerations of aesthetics and drama have simply swept information aside. Figures 8 and 9, for example, reprint two pictorial displays—one hesitates to call them graphs or charts—from a recent "atlas of human sexual behavior."

The graphic shown in Figure 8 uses cloudlike shapes to present data on how often young men and women think about sex, with smaller clouds representing smaller percentages. (Why clouds? We can't be sure—the original graphic appears over a rough map of the southern hemisphere, so perhaps they are supposed to be clouds in the sky, or perhaps they are meant to evoke the cloudlike shapes that cartoonists use to denote unspoken thoughts.) But the cloud sizes are not remotely proportional to the numbers being represented. For example, 67 percent is nearly three and a half times greater than 19 percent, but the 67 percent cloud is many times larger than the 19 percent cloud. The graph actually makes it harder to visualize the scale of differences among the various numbers. (Although it's difficult

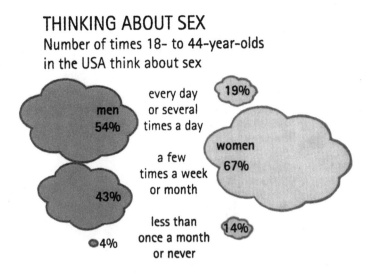

THINKING ABOUT SEX
Number of times 18- to 44-year-olds
in the USA think about sex

men
54%

every day
or several
times a day

19%

women
67%

a few
times a week
or month

43%

less than
once a month
or never

4%

14%

FIGURE 8. A graph in which visual proportions are unrelated to the numbers being represented. (*Source:* Judith Mackay, *The Penguin Atlas of Human Sexual Behavior* [New York: Penguin, 2000], p. 21; graphics © 2000 Myriad Editions, Ltd., used by permission of Viking Penguin.)

to tell, given the irregular shapes of the clouds, the creators of this graphic may have committed the classic error of making the clouds' width and height proportional to the numbers they represent.[11] The problem is that our eye does not see width and height but total area: if cloud B is twice as wide and twice as tall as cloud A, cloud B's area looks four—not two—times larger than cloud A's.)

Even worse is the display "Alcohol Impedes Pregnancy," shown in Figure 9. The data, which are very simple, show that women who drink more have somewhat greater difficulty becoming pregnant. Whereas 64 percent of women who had fewer than five drinks per week became pregnant within six

ALCOHOL IMPEDES PREGNANCY
Percentage of women in Denmark,
with different weekly alcohol
consumptions, becoming
pregnant within six months of
discontinuing contraception.

Fewer than five drinks 64%

More than ten drinks 55%

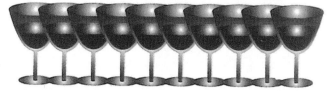

FIGURE 9. A visual display that graphs the scale instead of the data. (*Source:* Judith Mackay, *The Penguin Atlas of Human Sexual Behavior* [New York: Penguin, 2000], p. 47; graphics © 2000 Myriad Editions, Ltd., used by permission of Viking Penguin.)

months after stopping use of contraception, only 55 percent of those who reported having more than ten drinks per week became pregnant within the same period.

To illustrate these data, we are given rows of wineglasses. The 64 percent pregnancy rate among the women who drank less is represented by five wineglasses, while the 55 percent pregnancy rate among heavier drinkers gets ten wineglasses. At first glance, this is confusing—why use the smaller image to represent the higher pregnancy rate? But then all becomes clear: fewer than five drinks gets five glasses; ten or more drinks gets ten glasses. This must be a graphic for people (perhaps heavy drinkers?) who need help visualizing that five drinks are fewer than ten. It harkens back to those cave drawings where shepherds who lacked written numbers supposedly kept track of their flocks by drawing one sheep for each animal. Of course, by choosing to represent the independent variable (that is, the number of drinks) rather than the dependent variable (the pregnancy rates), the graphic in Figure 9 abandons any effort to convey information.

Selectivity

Overall, aesthetic considerations seem to cause much of the mischief in contemporary graphs. We should also recognize the possibility that graphs' creators may deliberately manipulate aesthetics in an effort to slant their presentations, but we need not jump to this interpretation. Remember, the standard graphics software programs adopt default options, such as truncated vertical scales, that guarantee distortion. Moreover, many bad graphs seem to lack any agenda. Even if we agree that the pie chart in Figure 4, the graduation cap in Figure 6, and the clouds and wineglasses in Figures 8 and 9 constitute poor graphics practices, it is hard to detect a deceptive intent behind those incoherent displays.

In other cases, however, the choices made about how to present data seem intended to reinforce a particular argument. Every graphic—like every statistic—reflects a series of choices: What will be shown? How will it be displayed? Some selectivity is inevitable, but this necessity can be abused.

In Figure 10, we can see two lines on a graph—a pretty good graph—from a government publication on the birth rate among teenagers. One line tracks the birth rate (that is, the number of births per 1,000 women in the age group) over the second half of the twentieth century. Although the line shows some fluctuations, it is apparent that the birth rate among teenagers ages fifteen to nineteen generally declined during this time: it peaked in 1957, at 96.3 births per 1,000, but was only 48.7 in 2000, "the lowest level ever reported for the Nation."[12] This might seem surprising, given the frequency with which the media carry alarmed stories about teen pregnancies and births.

But consider the second line, which reports the percentage of teen births involving unmarried mothers. In 1957, only 13.9 percent of teen births were to an unmarried teenager, but this figure rose to 78.7 percent in 1999. That is, even as the teen birth rate has been falling, the percentage of births to unmarried teenagers has been rising. The problem is not that the birth rate among teenagers has been increasing—it has not. Rather, the concern is that a growing share of the births that do occur are to unmarried teenagers, who often find it more difficult to support and care for their children. In previous decades, couples married earlier (sometimes because the bride was pregnant); today, marriage tends to be postponed, even when a pregnant woman decides to give birth.

So what should we think about trends in teen births? Neither line tells the complete story. We might read the declining trend

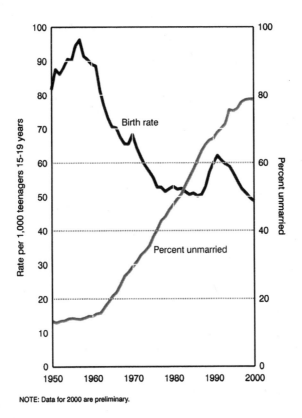

FIGURE 10. The two lines in this graph tell a complicated story. (*Source:* Stephanie J. Ventura, T. J. Mathews, and Brady E. Hamilton, "Births to Teenagers in the United States, 1940–2000," *National Vital Statistics Reports* 49, no. 10 [September 25, 2001]: 2.)

in the teen birth rate as indicating that things are getting better, but at least some critics would view the growing proportion of births to unmarried teens as evidence of things getting worse. In this case, the numbers are not wrong or deceptive; both lines in the graph are based on very good data (federal compilations of all reported births). But neither line by itself conveys a clear understanding of what's happening; we need to look at the two lines together to get a better overall sense of the complex ways society is changing.

But it is easy to imagine advocates who might want to promote a particular point of view about teen pregnancy—that it either does or doesn't represent a crisis—and who selectively choose to present a graph with only one of these lines (the one that supports their perspective). Which trend these advocates decide to highlight—the declining teen birth rate or the rising percentage of births to unmarried teens—is likely to shape how we think about this issue.

Similarly, it makes a difference how much data are displayed. Although Figure 10 shows that the teen birth rate generally declined from 1950 to 2000, we can note that the rate did not change very much from roughly 1975 to 1985. The birth rate then rose sharply between 1986 and 1991, before falling somewhat below the previous lows. Consider how the shape of the graph would change if advocates presented data only from 1975 to 1985, from 1985 to 1991, or even from 1975 to 2000. This variation suggests that we should be careful about making too much of graphs that display only short-term changes, which may turn out to be nothing more than unimportant fluctuations in a fairly steady long-term trend.[13] It is always worth asking whether data might have been carefully selected to promote a particular argument and whether other data exist that might support other interpretations. The example of data on teenage births ought to remind us that social issues are complex and multifaceted, not one-dimensional.

The sorts of confusion discussed in this chapter are particularly unfortunate because they are so unnecessary. Percentages and pie charts are relatively simple tools; most of us first encounter them in elementary school. Perhaps their very familiarity helps lull us into complacency—we assume that we understand completely and fail to recognize our confusion. Or perhaps we suddenly realize that there's something wrong with the numbers ("that can't be true, can it?!"), but we can't figure out where the mistake lies. Confusion fosters frustration, the sense that this stuff is just too complicated, which in turn leads to surrender ("I'll never get it, so there's no point in trying").

But we do have an alternative. Instead of declaring ourselves powerless, we can spend a few moments trying to understand what might be wrong. Is a graph confusing? Examine it. What is being represented, and how are those numbers being translated into pictures? Do the visual proportions accurately reflect the numbers? Is key information missing? What would you like to know that isn't shown? Remember that graphs are supposed to make things clear; if you're confused, it may well be the fault of the graph itself.

Similarly, basic statistics—averages, percentages, and the like—should be fairly easy to comprehend. If you're confused or shocked by what the numbers show, give some thought to what those numbers mean. Where do those figures come from? Who produced them, why did they go to the trouble of doing so, and how did they go about the task? Would it make a difference if the numbers were calculated or presented in different ways?

It might not be possible to answer some of these questions, but even that can be useful information. If we haven't been told enough to answer our basic questions, it's a sign that there's something wrong. If it seems that the numbers are steering us toward a particular point of view, we ought to ask why those numbers have been chosen. We can learn to treat confusion as a challenge rather than as a sign that we should surrender.

A series of recent polls asked American adults to estimate the percentage of children without health insurance and to describe recent trends in the teenage crime rate, the teenage birth rate, and the percentage of children raised in single-parent families.[1] A clear pattern emerged: on each of these issues, large majorities—between 74 and 93 percent of the respondents—judged that the problems were worse than they actually were. For example, 76 percent responded that the percentage of children living in single-parent families had increased during the previous five years. In fact, the percentage had not changed. Some 66 percent responded that the percentage of teens committing violent crimes had increased during the previous ten years, and another 25 percent said that the percentage had remained about the same; but there had actually been a decrease. What accounts for this tendency to imagine that things are worse than they are?

Because statistics can be confusing, they make most of us a little anxious. In addition, many of the numbers we encounter are intended, if not to scare us, at least to make us anxious about our world. Of course, most of what counts as newsworthy is bad news; our local "happy news" broadcast may end with a forty-five-second piece about a skydiving grandmother, but the lead story often features a reporter at the scene of a fatal convenience store robbery. The same pattern holds for statistics: in general, disturbing, scary statistics get more news coverage than numbers reporting good news or progress. It's no wonder we tend to exaggerate the scope of social problems. We're used to a fairly steady stream of statistics telling us what's wrong, warning that things are much worse than we might imagine.

This tendency to highlight scary numbers reflects the way social problems become noticed in our society. Advocates seeking to draw attention to a social problem must compete with other causes for the notice of the press, politicians, and the public. Amid a cacophony of competing claims, advocates must make the case that their particular problem merits concern. Their claims tend to hit familiar notes: the problem is widespread; it has severe consequences; its victims are vulnerable and need protection; everyone is a prospective victim; the problem is getting worse. Evidence to support these claims often comes from coupling troubling examples (as discussed in chapter 1) with statistics. Advocates seeking to raise concern naturally find it advantageous to accentuate the negative; therefore, they prefer scary statistics that portray the problem as very common or very serious.

But advocates aren't the only ones favoring frightening figures. The media comb the most routine statistical reports, such as the release of census figures, for their most newsworthy—

usually understood to mean the most troubling—elements. And, as we will see in chapter 4, even scientists and officials may find that emphasizing scary numbers makes their work seem more important.

DESCRIBING SOCIAL PROBLEMS IN SCARY TERMS

When advocates describe a social problem, the statistic we're most likely to hear is probably some sort of estimate of the problem's size—the number of cases or the number of people affected, for example. Large numbers support claims that the problem is common and therefore serious. Other statistics, such as the number or percentage of people victimized, convey a sense of risk; they offer a rough estimate for the likelihood that the problem will threaten you or someone you love. These figures foster a sense of our vulnerability. Still other statistics, such as rates of growth, project the problem into the future, leading us to believe that what is now bad is likely to become much worse.

Such statistics are most compelling when they portray the world in especially frightening terms. The more widespread the perceived harm and suffering, the more likely it seems that the problem will impinge on our world; and the greater the prospects for things getting worse, the greater our fear. This fear, in turn, makes the advocates' claims seem more compelling and therefore more likely to influence us. Whereas earlier generations of reformers spoke of society's moral obligation to aid its most vulnerable and most wretched members, contemporary claims often encourage people to act out of self-interest. We democratize risk by warning that a problem can touch anyone. "NOW NO ONE IS SAFE FROM AIDS" was the message on *Life* magazine's July 1985 cover; another sound bite from the same era claimed that "many families are just a couple of paychecks away from homelessness." Saying that everyone is vulnerable implies that everyone is *equally* vulnerable; such claims downplay well-documented patterns of risk in favor of fostering a shared sense of danger. If we see AIDS or homelessness affecting some other segment of society, then advocates must appeal to our sense of moral obligation. But if a threat seems to endanger everyone, then we all have a vested interest in doing something about the problem. It is telling that modern persuasion so often invokes self-interest rather than concern for others.

Even when a problem does not appear to pose a direct, immediate threat, it is possible to paint a picture of a future when things will be much worse. Trends are a way of spotting troubling patterns; even if things aren't bad now, we may see signs that they are deteriorating. Of course, the most frightening trends are those that seem to lead inevitably toward catastrophe. Statistical estimates for future social problems are hard to contradict; aside from waiting to see how things turn out, it is difficult to debunk a doomsday scenario. Still, a glance at the recent history of prognostication reveals how cloudy experts' visions of the future can be. The popular magazines of my boyhood predicted that the world of 2000 would feature commuters traveling to work in atomic-powered cars and personal helicopters, yet they made no mention of personal computers. The track record of advocates envisioning the future of social problems is not much better: just recall those Y2K forecasts of the widespread social collapse that would follow the simultaneous failure of the world's computer systems as the calendar shifted from 1999 to 2000.

A tension exists, then, between advocates' need for compelling rhetoric—claims that can move others to address some social problem—and the limitations of the available evidence. Commonly, this is resolved by ignoring those limitations in favor of presenting the most powerful message. For activists, who believe firmly that their cause is right and who may well consider the numbers perfectly reasonable, scary statistics have obvious appeal. For the media, scary numbers seem newsworthy, the stuff of good stories. Such numbers thus encounter remarkably little resistance. This section examines three sorts of figures often used to make social problems seem scary: big estimates, troubling trends, and apocalyptic scenarios.

Measuring a Problem's Size

The simplest sort of scary number estimates the size of a social problem—the number of people involved, for example, or the cost in dollars. This seems straightforward: we have all counted things, so we naturally presume that someone must have counted something to come up with these numbers. If someone's count has produced a big number, we tend to assume that there must be a big problem.

But social problems are notoriously tricky to count. Cases may be hard to identify, and it may be difficult to define and measure whatever is being counted. Take recent heavily publicized claims that preventable medical errors kill between forty-four thousand and ninety-eight thousand U.S. hospital patients each year. These are remarkably scary numbers, both because they seem large and because we go to hospitals in the hope of preserving our lives, not ending them. But what, exactly, are medical errors that kill—and how might we identify them and count them? The fact that we are given a fairly wide range of numbers for the death toll reveals that these numbers are estimates, not precise counts. So how did people arrive at these figures?

The answer is a little complicated. These particular estimates were derived from two studies of hospital discharges that reviewed patients' records to identify "adverse events" (injuries caused by medical mistakes); the researchers concluded that about 3 to 4 percent of patients experienced such injuries. However, neither study measured the percentage of adverse events that were preventable or the percentage of preventable adverse events that led to death—both of these figures were later estimated by people who reinterpreted the data from the original studies.[2] These later estimates of deaths, not the original research on adverse events, were the statistics that attracted public attention, despite critics who argued that the basis for those estimates was not made clear.

In addition, the original studies did not consider the overall health of each patient. One later study adopted a more refined analysis that did consider this factor. The results of this research remind us that hospital patients are, after all, often very ill. Imagine a patient who is already seriously ill, who is not expected to live more than a few days. A medical error—even a "preventable adverse event"—might be the immediate cause of that patient's death; in fact, the precarious health of such patients makes them particularly vulnerable to the effects of medical mistakes. But such cases are not likely to be chosen to exemplify the danger of medical mistakes. Advocates and the media favor more melodramatic examples, pointing to patients who, prior to the adverse event, had long life expectancies—for example, a high school athlete whose surgery for a minor injury led to severe brain damage.[3] The study that took into account the overall health of each patient suggested that "optimal [that is, mistake-free] care . . . would result in roughly 1 additional patient of every 10,000 admissions living 3 months or more in good cognitive health."[4] In other words, these researchers argued, medical errors rarely kill patients with good life expectancies.

The point of this example is not to argue that hospitals don't make fatal errors—surely they do. Nor do I mean to dismiss some studies and endorse others. The point is that measures of a problem's size may not be nearly as straightforward as they seem. This example illustrates how tricky it can be to measure what might appear, at first glance, to be an unambiguous phenomenon—patients killed by medical errors. Even assuming (optimistically) that we can identify which deaths result from medical mistakes, should we count every fatal error? Some might answer that, certainly, every patient's death ought to count. But others might see a difference between an error that shortens the life of a comatose, terminally ill patient by a single day and one that robs a relatively healthy young person of decades of life. And does our sense of the problem change if we discover that cases of the latter sort are relatively rare?

There are no right answers to such questions; reasonable people can disagree about what ought to count. But such subtleties rarely figure into discussions of social problems, given the considerable rhetorical advantages of depicting a problem as being as large—and as scary—as possible. And, of course, using compelling examples to illustrate the problem can make the figures seem even more frightening.

Troubles with Trends

Even if a problem isn't all that large now, it may be growing. Measurements over time allow us to identify trends, that is, patterns of change. This is an important form of reasoning, but, again, it is not as straightforward as it might seem. The basic problem with assessing trends is maintaining comparable measurements: if we don't measure the same things in the same way on each occasion, our figures may reflect changes in how we count rather than changes in anything we are counting.[5]

One way of testing claims about social trends is to ask what might be causing the change. Suppose that the media announce that reports of, say, in-law abuse have been rising. Why, we should ask, might this be happening? Is there some reason to suspect that the number of in-laws involved in abuse is growing? Perhaps. But isn't it also possible that people are now paying more attention to in-law abuse? (Obviously this is true, as there are now news reports about the topic.) Maybe people are becoming more familiar with the problem, more likely to deem it serious, and therefore more likely to report it; and maybe the authorities, in turn, are doing a better job of keeping records of those reports. Advocates often dismiss such alternative explanations; they may argue that giving more attention to in-law abuse has created some sort of "backlash," with increased concern somehow causing more cases of abuse. Claims beget counterclaims, but the burden of proof must fall on those who argue that the trend exists.

A couple of guidelines suggest themselves. First, we should be suspicious of claims that trends have suddenly reversed direction. In general, social patterns change slowly because social arrangements have considerable inertia. Social networks are webs of connections, reinforced by sets of cultural assumptions. Neither those networks nor those assumptions are likely to change all at once. When we think about why some people commit crimes, it can help to also consider why most people's behavior, most of the time, is law-abiding. Criminologists offer all sorts of answers, focusing on family dynamics, the state of the economy, the nature of the criminal justice system, the messages conveyed by the larger culture, and so on. The incidences of criminality and law-abiding behavior may well depend on all of these. The very complexity of these causal linkages makes it harder for trends to suddenly shift: while one cause of crime might undergo a dramatic alteration, it is unlikely that all the causal factors will change at the same time. Despite this complexity, however, when people warn about some new trend, they tend to argue that a particular change in one specific factor is having a dramatic effect.

Even when new trends do emerge, simple one-variable explanations probably cannot account for the development. For example, after crime rates rose during the 1980s, they reversed direction and began falling during the 1990s. Various claims attributed the new trend to particular causes, such as the war on drugs, "broken-windows" policing (that is, strictly enforcing laws against public disorder), or more police on the streets. But criminologists who sought to investigate and explain the falling crime rates concluded that a combination of factors—including economic prosperity and changing patterns in drug use—was at work.[6]

Second, we should be suspicious of explanations that attribute a trend to some sort of anxiety produced by our fast-changing society. We do live in a world marked by more or less constant change, but this is nothing new. Since the Industrial Revolution (usually dated from the first half of the nineteenth century), change has been part of Americans' ongoing experience. When we marvel at how the Internet has speeded up communication, for example ("it's changed everything!"), we forget the dramatic transformations wrought by the spread of telephones in the twentieth century or the rise of telegraphy in the nineteenth. Concerns that the pace of change threatens to disrupt America's social fabric have been voiced for at least two centuries. Even when we have confidence in our ability to measure trends, we need to be wary of jumping to conclusions about their causes.

Apocalypse Soon?

Contemporary discussions of social problems frequently warn not only that troubling trends are getting worse but that terrible catastrophe awaits. These warnings take many forms: concerns about warfare spiraling out of control (nuclear war, nuclear winter, the hazards of chemical or biological weapons of mass destruction); environmental disasters (overpopulation, resource depletion, pollution, global warming); medical fears (epidemics of new diseases such as HIV or Ebola, medical problems caused by pollution); anxieties about economic collapse; and other exotic threats, from asteroid collisions and robotics (artificial intelligences that push people aside) to nanotechnology (engineered materials that outcompete biological life-forms)—and don't forget the Y2K crisis. It is, apparently, a dangerous world out there.

Needless to say, when apocalyptic visions feature statistics, the numbers usually lack precision. Often, the method adopted is the one pioneered by Thomas Malthus, the eighteenth-century parson who explained that famine was inevitable because population growth must outstrip agricultural production. Malthus's model was simple and easily understood; anyone who accepts its assumptions must conclude that the outcome—catastrophic famine—is unavoidable. The only problem is that Malthus's assumptions have proven wrong: population growth can be and has been controlled in society after society (most experts expect global population to stop growing sometime during this century), and agricultural production has in fact expanded faster than the population.

The lesson is that apocalyptic scenarios—and especially those that are more than fantastic ("hey, it could happen!")—depend on their assumptions. The accuracy of those assumptions has everything to do with whether the scenario is worth our worry. The world is very complicated, more complicated than the most elaborate computer models. Yet, when we talk about social problems—even huge problems that might threaten life as we know it—we tend to reduce complexity to simplicity.

I certainly lack the knowledge to assess the scientific basis for warnings about global warming—and I suspect that most people who work for the news media aren't much better qualified. We depend on scientific experts to advise us on such matters. However, I do know enough—as should the folks in the media—to doubt that any single bit of evidence is sufficient to establish that catastrophic global warming is occurring. For example, a biologist's report that the range of the Edith's checkerspot, a California butterfly, had shifted northward led the press to treat this finding as important evidence of the impact of global warming. Later analyses questioned this interpretation, but the point is that evidence of a change in the habitat of a particular butterfly species isn't sufficiently compelling to either confirm or discredit the argument that human activity is causing potentially catastrophic global warming.[7] Surely there ought to be many, many such bits of evidence if claims about global warming are true. Yet news media tend to fix on such isolated reports: the stories are easy to understand (the butterflies have moved north); they lend themselves to illustration (we can imagine announcers speaking over videotaped butterflies fluttering); and they can be heralded as evidence of a larger, frightening trend.

Apocalyptic claims do not have a good track record. And assertions that statistics support such claims—particularly arguments that simple, easily understood numbers are proof that the future holds complex, civilization-threatening changes—deserve the most careful inspection.

RISKS

Risk statistics have become one of the most common types of scary numbers. We talk about "increased risk," "risk factors," or being "at risk." The watershed in our understanding of risk may have been the 1960s, a decade that included such landmark events as the release of the 1964 surgeon general's report on tobacco and health. While critics had long warned that smoking damaged health, the tobacco industry had insisted that no convincing evidence made this causal link. The surgeon general's report had great impact precisely because it seemed authoritative (although few Americans could have explained in any detail how the surgeon general had drawn the conclusions in the report) and because it claimed to offer a comprehensive overview of a large body of evidence that led to one conclusion: overall, smoking increased one's risk of contracting various diseases.

The surgeon general's report nearly coincided with the publication of two other famous risk-centered books. Rachel Carson's *The Silent Spring* (1962) warned that DDT and other chemicals threatened the environment, while Ralph Nader's *Unsafe at Any Speed* (1965) attacked the automobile industry's failure to design safer cars. These critiques portrayed everyday products—cigarettes, chemicals, and cars—as posing serious yet largely hidden dangers. Such analyses fostered discussions of risk. By the decade's end, a consumer rights movement had emerged that sought protection against hazardous products, and the environmental movement had attracted new support by emphasizing the dangers posed by pollution. Increasingly, risks were understood as hidden, perhaps unrecognized, and dangerous—yet potentially manageable if properly understood, acknowledged, and addressed. By warning the public about these risks, the news media had a vital role in this process.

Many of the trappings of modern life—seat belts; automobile air bags; bicycle helmets; foods produced without fat, caffeine, or pesticides; smoke-free restaurants and workplaces; safe sex; daily baby aspirins; assorted medical check-ups—reflect our current understanding of, and efforts to minimize, various risks. There is a comic quality to some of this, as we try to adjust our lives to the latest news story about the latest study. Is drinking bad for your health, or is a daily drink beneficial, or is it just red wine that's good for you? (Personally, I'm clinging to the notion that dark chocolate prolongs life, and if you have convincing evidence to the contrary, I don't want to hear it.)

When we try to translate these words into numbers, we enter the realm of probability. A risk is the chance, the probability, that something might occur. Thus, when we say that smokers have a higher risk of developing lung cancer, we are not saying that every smoker will develop lung cancer, nor are we saying that no nonsmoker will develop the disease. Rather, the notion of increased risk implies comparing probabilities: if X of every 1,000 nonsmokers eventually develop lung cancer, and if smokers develop the disease at a higher rate, then the number of lung cancer cases per 1,000 smokers should be markedly higher than X. The idea seems simple, but the numbers quickly lead to confusion.

Probability is not well understood. (This explains why casinos flourish.) We tend to recognize patterns and assume that they are meaningful. If we flip a fair coin four times and get four straight heads, some people assume that the next flip will be tails (because this outcome is somehow "overdue"), while others assume that it will be heads (because there is a "streak" going). A mathematician would say that both assumptions are wrong because each coin flip is independent of the others; that is, what happens on the next flip is not influenced by what happened on the previous flip. After four straight heads, the odds of heads on the fifth flip remain fifty-fifty. Should we get a fifth consecutive heads, the odds of heads on the sixth flip are still fifty-fifty. If we flip a coin a total of six times, we have sixty-four possible sequences of results. Six consecutive heads (HHHHHH) is one of those results; HTHTHT is another. We tend to notice the former and consider it remarkable, while the latter seems routine, but the odds of getting either pattern are exactly the same: one in sixty-four. This is not to say that the odds of getting six heads are the same as the odds of getting three heads and three tails; twenty of the sixty-four possible sequences involve three heads and three tails (HHHTTT, HHTHTT, and so on), whereas only one of the sixty-four sequences involves six heads. But any particular sequence is equally likely to occur, and the fact that some sequences seem to form recognizable patterns does not make them any more or less likely to occur.

Once we realize this, we can understand that all sorts of apparently unusual combinations—the sorts of things we might consider remarkable coincidences—can be expected to occur on occasion. If about 10 percent of people are left-handed, then the odds that the next person we see will be left-handed are one in ten (or .1), the odds are one in a hundred that the next two people will both be left-handed (.1 × .1 = .01), and one in a thousand that the next three people will be lefties (.1 × .1 × .1 = .001). Despite these odds, if we meet lots of people, we will occasionally run into two or even three consecutive left-handers. Even rare things can be expected to happen—it's just that they will happen rarely.

Converting these principles into statistics—risk calculations—routinely leads to confusion. Consider the following word problem about women receiving mammograms to screen for breast cancer (the statements are, by the way, roughly accurate in regard to women in their forties who have no other symptoms):

The probability that one of these women has breast cancer is 0.8 percent. If a woman has breast cancer, the probability is 90 percent that she will have a positive mammogram. If a woman does not have breast cancer, the probability is 7 percent that she will still have a positive mammogram. Imagine a woman who has a positive mammogram. What is the probability that she actually has breast cancer?[8]

Confused? Don't be ashamed. When this problem was posed to twenty-four physicians, exactly two managed to come up with the right answer. Most were wildly off: one-third answered that there was a 90 percent probability that a positive mammogram denoted actual breast cancer; and another third gave figures of 50 to 80 percent. The correct answer is about 9 percent.

Let's look carefully at the problem. Note that breast cancer is actually rather rare (0.8 percent); that is, for every 1,000 women, 8 will have breast cancer. There is a 90 percent probability that those women will receive positive mammograms—say, 7 of the 8. That leaves 992 women who do not have breast cancer. Of this group, 7 percent will also receive positive mammograms—about 69 cases of what are called false positives. Thus, a total of 76 (7 + 69 = 76) women will receive positive mammograms, yet only 7 of those—about 9 percent—will actually have breast cancer. The point is that measuring risk often requires a string of calculations. Even trained professionals (such as doctors) are not used to calculating risk and find it easy to make mistakes.

Unfortunately, these same doctors may give exactly this sort of information about risk to their patients—who have far less training, and may be upset in the bargain. A woman who has a positive mammogram is likely to be very troubled by that news and will probably be even less able to sort through the numbers and calculate the overall risk than the physicians were (who, remember, mostly bungled the answer).

Measuring Risks

But how do we calculate risks? Where do they get those figures? This is a tricky question. Ideally, science proceeds through
experiment. Suppose that we want to learn whether some activity—say, drinking diet cola (something I do often)—poses a
health risk. We can imagine a fantastic experimental design in
which we take two randomly assigned groups of children and
raise them in identical circumstances, except that the experimental group drinks diet cola and the control group does not.
We follow them through adulthood into old age and determine
whether the groups have different sorts of health problems.
Obviously, it would be impossible to conduct this experiment—
it would be ridiculously costly in time and money, to say nothing of its unethical interference with the subjects' lives. For
these reasons, risk calculations almost never derive from experiments with human subjects.

Instead, researchers must devise alternative methods for
studying risk. For example, they may identify sick people and
see whether those who are ill report drinking more diet cola
than people who are well, or they may compare rates of illness
in communities known to have high and low rates of diet cola
drinking, or they may conduct experiments in which some lab
rats drink diet cola and others don't. All of these designs involve
methodological compromises; they are imperfect ways of determining whether diet cola drinkers run greater risks of ill health.
On the one hand, this is inevitable; every piece of scientific research contains design limitations. On the other hand, the im-
perfections in measuring risk are particularly glaring (because it
is never possible to study humans under strictly controlled, ex-

perimental conditions), and therefore the results of these analyses are imprecise and need to be treated with great care. Two cautions are particularly important.

First, research results should not be treated as compelling unless they reveal substantial risk. Imagine a study in which subjects who drink diet cola are found to be more likely to experience a particular disease than subjects who never touch the stuff. Since our study cannot possibly have controlled for every aspect of these people's lives, we cannot know for sure that drinking diet cola caused the difference. To use the term introduced in chapter 2, the relationship between diet cola and this disease may be spurious. For example, we might suspect that diet cola drinkers are more likely to be concerned about their weight. Perhaps they get less exercise, or eat more, or are genetically predisposed to weight gain. How can we be sure that their health problems are a result of their choice of drink rather than a result of one or more of these other factors? We can't be sure. Therefore, before we jump to the conclusion that diet cola is the cause of the higher incidence of disease among cola drinkers, we ought to have fairly strong evidence.

But what constitutes strong evidence? A common standard in this sort of epidemiological research requires that identified risks be three times those in the comparison group (that is, 200 percent greater). (Confused? If X is 5, then three times X is 15, which is 10 greater than 5. Since 10 is 200 percent of 5, 15 is three times—or 200 percent greater than—5.) This is not an arbitrary standard. Because such research is not truly experimental, it is easy to suspect that apparently causal relationships might be spurious. And the weaker the relationship, the more likely that it is just an accidental finding, particularly if the risk being studied is rare. According to statistical theory—too technical to explain here—the chances that an apparent relationship (involving a rare risk) is not actually valid diminish only when the identified risks are at least 200 percent greater.[9]

Understanding even this much gives us a powerful tool for evaluating press reports of recent research. Suppose that you pick up tomorrow's newspaper and read that a medical journal has published a study indicating that diet cola drinkers are 20 percent more likely to have a specific medical condition. Such a sentence will confuse some people, who, for example, may now believe that 20 percent of diet cola drinkers will get this disease. Actually, this statistic means nothing of the sort.

Let's assume that, in the general population, 5 people in 10,000 have the disease. If diet cola drinkers have a 20 percent increased risk, there would be 6 cases of the disease among every 10,000 diet cola drinkers (20 percent of 5 is 1, so a 20 percent increased risk would equal 5 + 1, or 6). In other words, what might seem to be an impressive statistic—"20 percent greater risk!"—actually refers to a very small difference in the real world: 1 additional case per 10,000 people. (In fact, we can suspect that researchers and media coverage favor the wording "20 percent greater" over "a 1.2 risk factor," which means the same thing, precisely because it makes the result seem bigger and more dramatic.)

But remember: to be taken seriously, the research ought to report a 200 percent greater risk. For example, if the rate is 5 cases of disease per 10,000 in the general population, the research should reveal a disease rate of at least 15 cases per 10,000 among diet cola drinkers (15 is three times—200 percent greater than—5). Is this a reasonable standard? Well, smokers are about 1,900 percent more likely to develop lung cancer than nonsmokers.

Any time you read a news story that reports a risk of less than three times, or 200 percent, greater, you have every reason to be skeptical of the results.

As a second caution, we should insist on multiple studies. Any single study can be mistaken. Scientists know that to test the validity of findings, it must be possible to replicate the research—to repeat the study and get similar results. (The bubble of excitement over the reported discovery of cold fusion in 1989 collapsed precisely because researchers in other laboratories were unable to replicate the reported results.) It also helps to triangulate research, that is, to study a phenomenon using different methods. Although any one method has its own flaws, the different flaws in the various methods can cancel out one another. The link between smoking and lung cancer, for example, is considered well established because it has been consistently supported in studies that use a variety of methods.

Sometimes researchers compare the results of several studies in what is called meta-analysis. The logical assumption is that if several studies consistently show an effect, even if the effect is not powerful (that is, the risk is less than the 200 percent greater standard), the multiple consistent results ought to give us more confidence that the relationship is real. The problem with this logic is that researchers often do not seek to publish—or have greater difficulty publishing—disappointing results. This *publication bias* means that it is hard to get studies with weak results published. Thus, meta-analyses tend to include only the most successful studies—those with results strong enough to get published. While the meta-analysis technique is not illegitimate, neither does it provide particularly strong support. A meta-analysis of several studies showing, say, 20 percent greater risk should not fill us with confidence in the results.

It also helps to put risks in some larger context. Every time we get in a car and drive to work, we take a risk. We all understand that traffic accidents kill people. To some degree, we can minimize our risk by obeying the traffic laws and wearing our seat belts, but the risk never becomes zero, although the chance of being killed on any particular journey is very low. Still, such routine risks—the sorts of things we take for granted—may be far greater than the highly publicized risks that suddenly become the focus of public attention. When we are frightened, we tend to focus on what scares us rather than on the actual risk of our being affected, a reaction that has been termed "probability neglect."[10]

We can see a good example of this in the public's alarmed reaction to the news that a sniper was killing people in the region around Washington, D.C., during the fall of 2002. Because our ordinary, day-to-day assumption is that the risk of being shot by a sniper is zero, the news that some risk existed frightened people. Still, in a region containing millions of people, the risk of being shot remained very low. Even during the weeks when individuals died at the hands of the sniper, people were at much greater risk of dying in traffic accidents in greater Washington—yet traffic deaths were not headline news. Following the mundane advice we've heard all our lives—don't smoke, wear seat belts, eat sensibly, and exercise—is likely to increase our life expectancies far more than ducking to keep out of a sniper's sights or avoiding that food additive that figures so prominently in this week's headlines.

The Risk of Divorce

Another reason that the notion of risk leads to confusion is that we're not always sure how best to calculate risks. Consider an apparently simple question that turns out to be somewhat complicated: what proportion of marriages end in divorce? No official agency keeps track of particular marriages and is therefore able to identify precisely which ones end in divorce—which is the sort of information one would like to have to answer this question. Lacking complete and perfect data, analysts are forced to use the numbers that are available. Since filing a marriage license and obtaining a divorce are both legal steps, official agencies do keep records of these events, and various jurisdictions tally the marriages and divorces they record. Therefore, analysts have long divided the number of divorces during a particular year by the number of marriages during that year to get a rough measure of the likelihood of marriage ending in divorce. Since roughly 1960, the number of divorces has been nearly half that of marriages, and commentators often refer to this as the "divorce rate."

The problem is that when we speak of a rate, we are usually dividing some number of events (such as deaths or crimes) by the population at risk. Thus, both death rates and crime rates are usually presented as the number per 100,000 people in the population; for example, the FBI reported that the murder rate was 5.5 murders for every 100,000 people in the United States in 2000. But who makes up the population at risk when we try to calculate a divorce rate? Obviously, it does not include only those who married during the same year; in fact, we know that relatively few couples get divorced during the calendar year in which they marry. Rather, the population at risk is all married couples—a very large number indeed. If we calculate the rate of divorce by dividing the number of divorces during a particular year by the total number of married couples, regardless of the length of their marriages, then the divorce rate must be far less than 50 percent. All manner of commentators have made this point, insisting that marriage is therefore a more stable institution and divorce is less common than we might have imagined.

But let's examine this assertion. Imagine a community that records two marriages each year—and one of those new marriages ends in divorce during that same year. In this case, it is true that half of all new marriages end in divorce; yet it is also true that, with each passing year, the total number of married couples will grow by one. Thus, after the first year, dividing the current year's lone divorce by the total number of married couples will produce a rate lower than 50 percent in spite of the fact that half of marriages end in divorce. This reasoning suggests that the standard critique used to dismiss high divorce rate statistics must be flawed.

Clearly, measuring the risk of divorce is a tricky problem, one that requires both careful thought and, it turns out, a lot of data. In 1996, investigators interviewed a very large sample, nearly seventy thousand people at least fifteen years old, living in some thirty-seven thousand households. The respondents were asked about all marriages and divorces in their personal histories. For instance, one person might report marrying once, forty years earlier, and remaining married to the same spouse; whereas another respondent, currently unmarried, might report marriages in 1970 and 1985 that ended in 1980 and 1992, respectively.[11] These data allowed the investigators to identify cohorts of marriages that had occurred during different periods (for example, first marriages that took place in 1945–1949) and to calculate the proportion of marriages in each cohort that had ended in divorce by 1996. (It is always possible that a couple still married at the time of the interview could later decide to divorce.) Although these data are not complete, because they come from a sample rather than from the population as a whole, the sample is a good one—about as good as samples get—and the data give a glimpse of what happens to particular marriages over time (which was, remember, the sort of data we wished for at the beginning of this discussion).

Alas, these data suggest that about half of current marriages can be expected to end in divorce. The researchers found important cohort differences that reveal how society has changed; basically, people in each cohort were likely to have remained married longer than those in the cohort that followed. Thus, only about 34 percent of sixty-year-old men had had their first marriage end in divorce, but the comparable figure for fifty-year-old men was 40 percent. Of the women who first married during 1945–1949, 70 percent were still married thirty years later; but among those whose first marriage occurred during 1960–1964, only 55 percent (just over half!) remained married. It is too soon to tell what proportion of couples first married during 1980–1985 will celebrate their thirtieth anniversaries, but we can make projections based on the record so far: only 73 percent of the women who wed during those years were still married ten years later, compared to the 90 percent of those first married in 1945–1949 whose marriages lasted at least ten years. Based on these data, the investigators projected that, while a larger proportion of earlier marriages remained intact, about half of recent marriages will indeed end in divorce.

Thus, answering an apparently simple question—what is the likelihood that a marriage will end in divorce?—turns out to be a fairly complicated matter. But this sort of complexity is glossed over in media reports that glibly report on the risk of this or that—an observation that should give us pause. It is all too easy to be frightened by risk statistics. We need to keep in mind the difficulties of calculating risks as we digest today's warning about a newly discovered threat.

TRADE-OFFS AND PRESUMPTIVE PESSIMISM

Most often, scary numbers warn that our world is changing. It can be unsettling, even frightening, to think about change, particularly since media reports tend to focus on changes that are for the worse. One of the most useful ideas when considering the meaning of change is the notion of trade-off—that is, every change involves both costs and benefits. It is impossible to make a fair comparison between what came before and what follows unless we consider the comparable costs and benefits.

One of the classic methods of promoting a specific change is to contrast the costs of what we have now with the benefits the proposed change will bring; similarly, change can be resisted by emphasizing the benefits of the existing situation and the prospective costs that will be imposed. To protect ourselves—to make a fair comparison—we need to compare apples and apples. In other words, if we consider today's benefits relevant, we must compare them to future benefits, and today's costs ought to be compared to future costs.

It is surprisingly easy to forget to do this. Many critics have become suspicious of technological change and point to its costs. The comparison, which is often implicit, harkens back to an idyllic past when people somehow lived in harmony with nature, when life was simpler and better. This view through the mists of time is a little fuzzy; the critics can see the benefits of the past but have trouble making out the costs it entailed. Thus, they calculate the costs of, say, deaths caused by air pollution from modern power plants, but they forget to tally the death toll from indoor pollution caused by cooking over woodstoves. The critics' comparison usually involves weighing present or future deaths caused by change against a past in which, somehow, death is taken for granted. The opposite error occurs when boosters highlight the benefits of a proposed change and ignore its costs.

Comparisons that ignore trade-offs, along with big estimates, frightening trends, apocalyptic scenarios, and ill-defined risks, are among the most common ways of making statistics scary. Because scary numbers are compelling, and because we often have difficulty sorting out relative risks and trade-offs, a pessimistic presumption that things must be getting worse runs through many contemporary discussions of social problems.

These gloomy warnings contrast with the lived experiences of most Americans. I don't want to imply that every individual's world gets better every day in every way; our society features plenty of hardship and suffering. However, on average, Americans are living longer than their ancestors, they are healthier and better educated, and they have higher standards of living.[12]

There is, in short, a gap between our sense that our own lives are going pretty well and our perception that the larger society is beset by troubles. This gap regularly appears when public opinion polls ask pairs of questions about individuals' own experiences and their perceptions of the state of the nation. People tend to be reasonably satisfied with the teaching provided by their local schools but deeply concerned about the quality of American education; they often think pretty well of their local congressional representative but view Congress as a sinkhole; and they report being pleased with the directions their own lives are taking, even as they worry that society is on the wrong path. Presumptive pessimism colors our thinking about the larger society. As a professor, I have read thousands of term papers and examination essays over the years, and I realize that many students simply assume that crime (or poverty, or teen suicide) is getting worse, regardless of whether the actual crime rates are rising or falling. It is as though we all think of ourselves as living comfortably in Lake Wobegon (among all those above-average children), even while we are confident that the larger society is headed to hell in a handbasket.

In recent decades, we have been exposed to a variety of apocalyptic scenarios, warnings that life as we know it could end. Some threats have faded (remember the 1970s fears about a new ice age?), but we continue to hear about plenty of paths to extinction: nuclear winter, global warming, overpopulation, epidemic disease, economic collapse, terrorism. Scary statistics have an important place in these claims. Isolated findings, such as the report that a species of butterfly has shifted its habitat, can be presented as significant harbingers of impending disaster. Even good news can be interpreted as foretelling catastrophe: if crime rates are falling, the situation can't last; and should they stop falling, it is surely a sign that crime is about to swing back out of control. Our readiness to speculate about the largest possible implications of small developments means that we are constantly being warned that big things are in the offing. And, once more, we find ourselves frustrated by what seem to be contradictory claims—alcohol harms your health; no, a glass of red wine is good for you; no, a little alcohol in any form is good for your heart (but bad for your liver).

Scary numbers flourish because they are an integral part of the way we talk about social life. Advocates of different causes seek to scare us because, they insist, we face real threats and because we need to be jarred out of our comfortable complacency. They are less likely to acknowledge another consideration—the competition for our attention. We are surrounded by advocates for different causes, each group trying to get us to focus on a particular problem. Each cause hopes to stand out from the others. Frightening people is not the only way to win this competition, but it often works pretty well, especially if advocates can point to statistics to justify the fear. We have every reason to expect that scary numbers will remain a key feature of how we talk about social problems. These numbers aren't going to go away; all we can do is try to approach them with skepticism, to assess whether fear is really necessary.

A couple of times each month, I receive an e-mail message from the editor of some scholarly journal, asking whether I'd be willing to review a manuscript. Most people know that professors are under pressure to "publish or perish." Peer review is a largely hidden part of that publication process. Typically, after completing their research and writing reports about their findings, scholars submit their manuscripts to journals that specialize in publishing such articles. The editors of these journals receive more—sometimes far, far more—manuscripts than they can possibly publish, and they use peer review to help them choose among the submissions. The editor sends a copy of each manuscript to several reviewers (in sociology, the leading journals usually send copies to three or four reviewers). As the term suggests, these reviewers are supposed to be the researcher's peers—professionals knowledgeable about the topic and therefore qualified to judge the quality of a research report. Reviewers may disagree, but a journal's editor will almost always reject a manuscript that gets mostly negative reviews.

Authors, particularly those who have recently had manuscripts rejected, sometimes doubt the integrity of the review process. Some, for example, question whether reviews ought to be anonymous (they usually are, although authors and reviewers can often guess each other's identity); others raise suspicions that a negative review may reflect a reviewer's personal or political disagreements with an author. But the peer review process endures because it seems to work better than any other method for selecting the best scholarship for publication. It probably works best in the most prestigious journals. There are thousands of scholarly journals, but scholars in the various disciplines, specialties, and subspecialties recognize that some journals have far more readers than others; and competition to publish in the most widely read, and therefore most prestigious, venues is intense. Such journals are presumed to be especially selective.

Peer reviewers are gatekeepers. Their job is to identify a manuscript's flaws and call them to the editor's attention. Does an author seem unfamiliar with other recent research on the topic? Did the author choose questionable methods to conduct the study? Has the author used inappropriate techniques to analyze the research results? Reviewers' doubts on such points warn editors against publishing weak papers.

When people refer to a journal as "authoritative," they are speaking to the integrity of the journal's review process. Editors and reviewers cannot possibly oversee the entire research process and vouch for the accuracy of every word in a manuscript, but they can weigh what they read, be alert for warning signs, and allow only what seem to be the strongest papers to appear in print. Of course, mistakes occur. Over time, some published results are called into question; rarely, there is a dramatic exposé of scientific fraud—charges that researchers deliberately fudged their results to get their work published. But, overall, the system seems to work pretty well.

The authority of social institutions depends on such arrangements to ensure integrity. We design checks and balances, require officeholders to swear oaths, encourage ethics of professionalism, and devise other techniques to keep institutions and the people who fill them in line. To the degree that we have confidence in these arrangements, we can place our trust in, among other things, the statistics these institutions produce. When we are young children, most of us learn to be skeptical of claims (including statistics) that appear in advertisements; we come to expect them to be one-sided and distorted. In contrast, we have more confidence in statistics produced by scientists or government agencies. Such information is considered more authoritative because these institutions are presumed to be more professional, more impartial, and more committed to the accuracy of their numbers.

Thus, we can speak of *authoritative numbers,* statistics produced by those thought to be authorities, that reach us via institutional channels that seem to vouch for the accuracy of the figures. In general, these statistics avoid the clumsy errors discussed in earlier chapters. Numbers produced by authorities rarely involve mistakes in calculation; the methods of collecting and presenting the data are ordinarily appropriate. By the time most such statistics reach the public, they have been examined by colleagues, peer reviewers, editors, and others. These numbers are about as good as statistics get.

Nonetheless, even authoritative numbers need to be handled with care. This chapter examines some examples of statistics found in professional journals and government reports, in an effort to identify some of the sorts of questions that should be asked about such numbers. It begins with an extended discussion of an article in a major medical journal, a product of the peer review process.

HIGHLIGHTING RESULTS OF SCIENTIFIC RESEARCH

Each morning, I read the *Wilmington News Journal.* It is the principal newspaper in Delaware, but Delaware is not a big state, and other newspapers are much bigger than the *News Journal.* Still, it is a fairly typical contemporary newspaper. On April 25, 2001, a front-page *News Journal* story summarized an article that had appeared in that week's issue of the *Journal of the American Medical Association,* noting that "nearly one of every three U.S. children in sixth through 10th grades have been bullied, or bully other students themselves." Nor was this item unique. Two months later, the *News Journal* ran a story about another report in the *Journal of the American Medical Association* (more familiarly known as *JAMA*) headlined: "Sexual Solicitation Reported by 20% of Kids Who Use Web." And two months after that, a *News Journal* headline reported on yet another *JAMA* article: "1 in 5 Girls Abused by a Date, Study Suggests."[1]

The *News Journal* can't afford to pay a reporter to read through each week's issue of *JAMA* to locate newsworthy stories, so how does my local newspaper get these items? The answer is that it relies on wire services. But that raises another question: how do the wire services cover developments in science and medicine? *JAMA,* for instance, sends out press releases about articles in the current issue that its editors hope will prove newsworthy. (Not all scientific journals do this; *JAMA*'s principal rival for top medical journal honors, the *New England Journal of Medicine,* does not issue press releases to publicize its articles, although it does make advance copies of each issue available to the media.)[2]

Presumably, *JAMA* wants to get its name before the public, to give people the sense that it publishes important research. Among other things, *JAMA*'s visibility makes top researchers more eager to submit their research to the journal; publication there offers an opportunity to bring one's work to the notice of not only fellow professionals but also the larger public. And researchers who successfully place their papers in highly prestigious journals in turn please their funders—the government agencies or private foundations that supply the grants that pay for large-scale research. Knowing that their grants led to highly visible publications confirms to the funders that they spent their money wisely.

It is important to appreciate that this is an extremely competitive process. Funding agencies winnow through many grant applications to select those projects worthy of support. Would-be authors submit about ten times more manuscripts to *JAMA* than that journal can publish, and its editors must not only choose among these submissions but also decide which articles merit press releases. Newspapers are flooded with press releases and must determine which ones will run in the limited available space. By the time a piece of research finds its way into even a short item in the *News Journal,* it has survived several stages at which rejection is more likely than selection.

Remember that the *News Journal* published reports about *JAMA* articles indicating that bullying affected about 30 percent of students, that 20 percent of Internet-using youths had been sexually solicited, and that 20 percent of high school girls had been violently abused by dating partners. As an experiment, imagine that each of those articles had portrayed the problem it discussed as being one-tenth—or even one-third—as common; that is, imagine that bullying affected between 3 and 10 percent of students and that Internet sexual solicitations and dating violence each affected between 2 and 7 percent. The findings now seem less impressive, don't they? Would the *News Journal* still have published articles about those studies? Possibly—even probably—not. Would *JAMA*'s editors have circulated press releases for articles with those findings? Again, probably not. In fact, with those less impressive results, we can suspect that *JAMA*'s editors might have been less likely to publish those articles, that the authors might have been less likely to submit their papers to such a highly selective journal, and that the funding sources would have been less impressed with the reception given the published results. In other words, we can imagine that everyone in the publication process—the editors at the *News Journal* and at *JAMA,* the researchers, and the funders—might well prefer studies that produce more impressive numbers.

Let me be clear: I am not suggesting that anything fraudulent is involved in this process. True, rare scandals reveal that researchers have faked their results, but that is not what I'm describing. Rather, I'm simply suggesting that there are advantages to presenting research findings in terms that make the results seem as impressive as possible. A report depicting a big problem will be favored in the competition to gain attention.

So let's see how big numbers can be produced. Consider that study of bullying. The article in *JAMA*, "Bullying Behaviors Among U.S. Youth," presented results from a large representative sample of students (nearly sixteen thousand young people) in grades six through ten. The authors were associated with the National Institute of Child Health and Human Development, which supported the survey. The report received considerable coverage by print and broadcast news media, which featured the finding that nearly 30 percent of youths "reported moderate or frequent involvement in bullying." Researchers have conducted many other studies of bullying, but few have involved samples so large and well drawn. Given the composition and size of the sample, and the article's appearance in an especially prestigious journal, we might take it as representing the best work on the subject.

What, exactly, is bullying? According to one federal publication, "Bullying can take three forms: physical (hitting, kicking, spitting, pushing, taking personal belongings); verbal (taunting, malicious teasing, name calling, making threats); and psychological (spreading rumors, manipulating social relationships, or engaging in social exclusion, extortion, or intimidation)."[3] Anyone with clear memories of junior high school who reads that definition might be surprised that only 30 percent of the respondents in the *JAMA* study felt affected. *Bullying* is a term both broad and vague, and much of what might be classified as bullying is probably fairly common behavior.

Still, the proportion of students in a survey who report being involved in bullying will depend on the questions they are asked. The section dealing with bullying in the *JAMA* article's questionnaire began with an explanation:

Here are some questions about bullying. We say a student is *being bullied* when another student, or a group of students, say or do nasty and unpleasant things to him or her. It is also bullying when a student is teased repeatedly in a way he or she doesn't like. But it is *not bullying* when two students of about the same strength quarrel or fight. (emphasis in original)[4]

The students were then asked how frequently they bullied others or were bullied during the current school term. Separate questions covered bullying in and out of school, although those responses were combined for the *JAMA* article, which did not specify how much of the reported bullying occurred in schools. For each question, possible answers described different frequencies of involvement: "I haven't . . . ," "once or twice," "sometimes," "about once a week," and "several times a week." In presenting their results, the authors defined responses of at least weekly experiences as frequent involvement in bullying and responses of "sometimes" as moderate involvement.

These categories form the basis of the study's central finding, that nearly 30 percent of youths had moderate or frequent involvement in bullying. The authors conclude that "bullying is a serious problem for U.S. youth" and that "the prevalence of bullying observed in this study suggests the importance of preventive intervention research targeting bullying behaviors."[5] In other words, bullying is widespread, and something needs to be done about it.

But does the article demonstrate that bullying is a widespread, serious problem? The key statistic—that 30 percent of youths are involved in bullying—depends on three manipulations, three methodological choices. First, students could be involved either as a bully (13.0 percent acknowledged that they were bullies), a victim (10.6 percent), or both (6.3 percent). Choosing to count bullies as well as victims—that is, all of those "involved" in bullying—made a big difference; if the authors had chosen to count only the victims, their findings would have focused on about 17 percent of students (10.6 + 6.3 = 16.9), not on 30 percent.

Second, the authors included both "moderate" bullying (occurring "sometimes," that is, more than once or twice during the term but less than weekly) and "frequent" bullying (occurring at least weekly). Adopting a narrower definition would have made the findings seem less dramatic; only 8.4 percent of the respondents reported being targets of frequent bullying, not 17 percent.

Third, remember that the authors combined responses for questions about bullying in and outside school. Although the researchers did not report these data, at least some of those responding that they were frequently bullied might have identified this as happening only away from school. If so, even fewer than 8.4 percent would have reported frequent bullying in school. In other words, the authors made a series of choices that allowed them to estimate that bullying significantly affected 30 percent of students. Different choices—say, looking only at victims of frequent bullying in schools—would have produced a figure only about a quarter as large, if that.

The point is not that this is a bad piece of research, nor is it to deny that bullying may sometimes have serious consequences. (Some reports alleged that the shooters in heavily publicized school shootings were reacting to being bullied.) But the numbers that emerge from social research must be interpreted with care. The finding that 30 percent of students are involved in bullying needs to be understood not as some sort of absolute fact that has its own independent existence but rather as a product of a particular set of methodological decisions. How the survey's questions were worded, the order in which questions were asked, and the choices made in interpreting and summarizing the results for publication all shaped the findings. Similar methodological choices affected the well-publicized findings in the *JAMA* articles about Internet sexual solicitations and dating violence.

It is also important to understand the concerns that can underpin such research. An anti-bullying movement has arisen, which believes that bullying is a serious but neglected problem, one that must be addressed. Without such an expression of concern, the federal government might not have funded this costly, large-scale research. Of course, no well-established pro-bullying lobby exists; no one argues that bullying is desirable. Therefore, we can expect that most researchers studying the topic will seek to demonstrate that bullying is a serious problem—and that journal editors will prefer to publish articles that support that theme.

There was nothing dishonest or unprofessional about the *JAMA* piece. Anyone who reads the article will find all of the information I've presented in this discussion. But any article must be condensed to create an abstract or a press release; only a few of an article's many findings are highlighted when the piece is summarized. Emphasizing the 30 percent figure made this article seem more newsworthy, while other, less dramatic findings were ignored or downplayed in the press coverage. For example, the *JAMA* piece reveals that the percentages of students who reported that they had experienced bullying fell drastically as the students aged: 13.3 percent of sixth-graders but only 4.8 percent of tenth-graders said they experienced frequent bullying. Thus, bullying declines as youths mature—hardly a surprising finding, but one that might have implications for urgent calls for anti-bullying measures.

In exploring how the results of this study found their way onto the front page of my local newspaper, I mean to highlight the role of choices in shaping how research gets reported. All research is a product of a long series of choices. Analysts must determine what they want to study—a decision that may reflect such considerations as their own intellectual interests, their sense of what their colleagues consider worthwhile research, and the availability of funding. They must also make all manner of methodological choices: how to draw a sample and collect data, how to define and measure concepts, how to analyze and interpret the results. Research choices are constrained by what is already known and by the sorts of time, money, personnel, and other resources available for the study. But these choices are always consequential; they inevitably shape the results. Thus, every study has limitations; one can always argue that, had the analysts made different decisions, the findings might have been different. This is why scientists insist on both replicating research (repeating a study to confirm the results) and compiling bodies of findings from studies based on different choices. As the number of studies with consistent results grows, confidence in those findings swells.

But most of us do not closely follow the gradual expansion of scientific knowledge. Rather, we get our information about scientific advances from summaries of single studies that appear, say, on the front page of our daily paper. And the journalists who bring us those reports make choices, too: given all the stories competing for coverage, and given the limited number of newspaper column inches (or broadcast minutes) available, which stories merit coverage? With such constraints, the steady development of scientific knowledge doesn't seem especially compelling to reporters and editors, whereas an apparently pathbreaking piece of research seems like news. The news media look for drama or human interest. An article reporting that bullying is very common seems like a good story because a large share of the news audience may find the story relevant to their lives—audience members have children, or at least know children, and this makes the research seem interesting. (Of course, journals that issue press releases for their articles need to be aware of the media's concerns; a good press release should focus journalists' attention on a study's newsworthy aspects.)

To complicate matters, scientists have their own agendas: they generally want their research to appear in print, to receive recognition, and to lead to rewards such as tenure, promotion, and further grants. Some commentators tend to equate researchers' agendas with political ideologies, worrying that studies are designed to support liberal or conservative positions. But this is only a small part of the story. Researchers may also be allied with particular theoretical or methodological schools within their disciplines; for example, bitter debates may occur between factions favoring competing statistical models for interpreting research results. Such allegiances and concerns—largely hidden and incomprehensible to outsiders—often shape researchers' choices.

The scientific literature is supposed to be self-correcting. Scientists understand that no study is perfect, but they believe that, over time, the research process will produce a body of findings in which we can place our confidence. When researchers have reservations about a study's results, they may ask to examine the data and offer an alternative analysis, or they may decide to conduct a new study. Slowly, agreed-upon—that is, authoritative—knowledge emerges within the research community. But this process is slower and more complex than the way most of us consume the fruits of scientific research, via short news briefs that relay the contents of press releases.

AMBIGUITIES IN OFFICIAL RECORDKEEPING

Even the most professionally compiled data can be subject to misinterpretation. Consider death records. In the United States, the law requires completion of a death certificate for each known death; in each case, someone with authority, such as a physician or coroner, is expected to assign a cause of death. These records travel through bureaucratic channels until they eventually find their way to the National Center for Health Statistics. The NCHS, in turn, issues an annual report, *Vital Statistics of the United States,* summarizing records of births and deaths. The *Vital Statistics* reports once took the form of three phonebook-size volumes filled with huge, multipage tables; now the reports are in electronic form, and anyone can access them at the NCHS Web site. The federal government has been compiling these records for a long time, and most of the bugs have been worked out of the system. Counting births and deaths is relatively straightforward, and these data are about as complete and accurate—as authoritative—as any we might hope to find.[6]

And yet, misadventures are still possible. Consider reports of a late twentieth-century rise in suicides among African American teenagers. In 1998, the U.S. Centers for Disease Control and Prevention (CDC) reported that the suicide rate for African Americans between the ages of ten and nineteen more than doubled between 1980 and 1995 and that this increase was far greater than the increase among white youths.[7] This was a disturbing finding. Teen suicide strikes most adults as especially tragic, as an act expressing isolation, despair, and desperation. In addition, most Americans would like to think that race relations haven't been getting worse. Why would the suicide rate among black teens be rising near the end of the twentieth century?

Reporters who picked up on the CDC report tried to explain the apparent trend by contacting psychiatrists and clinical psychologists, the professionals usually considered the relevant experts; in effect, they own the suicide problem in our culture. These authorities mentioned a "post-traumatic slavery syndrome [that] can manifest itself in a range of self-destructive behavior." They also cited "family breakdown, low economic opportunities, undiagnosed depression, unacknowledged grief from neighborhood violence, even the additional stress of entering the middle class," in that "upwardly mobile black families may lack traditional family and community support."[8] The CDC report had suggested: "Black youths in upwardly mobile families . . . may adopt the coping behaviors of the larger society in which suicide is more commonly used in response to depression and hopelessness."[9] In other words, plenty of after-the-fact explanations were offered.

It is also possible, however, that the increase reflects not a change in black youths' behavior, but a change in how their

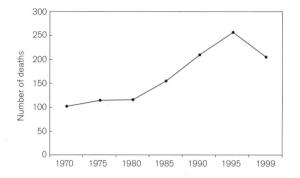

FIGURE 11. Suicides among African Americans ages ten to nineteen, 1970–1999. (*Source:* National Center for Health Statistics.)

deaths are processed by the authorities.[10] Consider Figure 11, which traces the number of suicides among African Americans ages ten to nineteen from 1970 through 1999. (In order to make the stages of my argument as clear as possible, I have chosen to graph the actual numbers of recorded deaths rather than the death rates. Presenting rates would not change the patterns in the data relative to the point of my argument.) As the graph in Figure 11 indicates, we are not talking about a lot of cases: according to the NCHS (which, remember, tries to record *all* deaths), there were slightly more than 100 suicides by black teens in 1970 and about 250 in 1995, whereas the 2000 census identified 6.2 million African Americans between the ages of ten and nineteen.

Figure 12 duplicates the first graph, but it adds a second line, showing the numbers of deaths in this age group that are listed as having an undetermined cause. In the NCHS listing, "undetermined" is a residual category for those few deaths that are not assigned a more specific cause. The comparison of the two

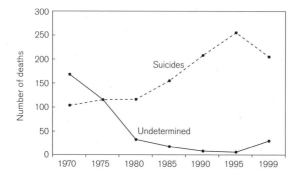

FIGURE 12. Suicides and deaths resulting from undetermined causes among African Americans ages ten to nineteen, 1970–1999. (*Source:* National Center for Health Statistics.)

lines is striking: as the number of suicides rose during the late twentieth century, the number of deaths resulting from undetermined causes fell.

Figure 13 adds another dimension to the analysis. It shows recorded deaths over the same period that were attributed to four accidental causes: drowning, gunshots, poison, and falls. I selected these four categories of fatal accidents because they are also common ways of committing suicide; for example, when an official completes a death certificate for a youth who drowned, the death might be recorded either as an accident or as a suicide. Figure 13 reveals that all four forms of accidental death declined among black youths during the last decades of the twentieth century.

Finally, Figure 14 combines all of the information from the three previous graphs into one bar graph. Each bar is broken into three segments: suicides on the bottom, deaths resulting from undetermined causes in the middle, and the four cate-

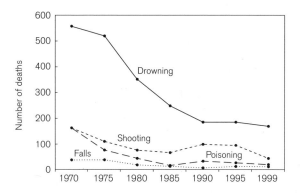

FIGURE 13. Accidental deaths resulting from drowning, shooting, poisoning, and falls among African Americans ages ten to nineteen, 1970–1999. (*Source:* National Center for Health Statistics.)

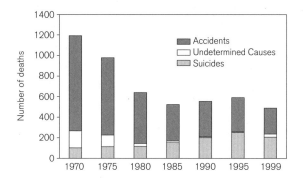

FIGURE 14. Deaths from four accidental causes, deaths from undetermined causes, and suicides among African Americans ages ten to nineteen, 1970–1999. (*Source:* National Center for Health Statistics.)

gories of accidental deaths on top. The total height of each bar represents, then, the total number of deaths attributed to all these causes. Again, we see that the number of suicides among black youths rose during this period, even as deaths from all of the other causes fell; overall, the total number of deaths from all of these causes dropped by more than half. This is important, because all of these deaths represent incidents that might conceivably be classified as suicides (depending, of course, on other available information). If anything, it is probably more difficult to classify a death as a suicide than to assign some other cause; because family members are more likely to resist a finding of suicide, it should be much easier to classify a death as accidental or even as a result of undetermined causes.

In other words, the rise in teen suicides among African Americans may not be all that mysterious. Its roots may reside not so much in, say, the psychological pressures on youths in upwardly mobile African American families as in a shift in the way officials handle the deaths of black teenagers. Whereas such deaths once may have been treated as relatively unimportant—perhaps brushed off as an accident or as a result of undetermined causes—officials may now conduct more careful investigations to arrive at the more difficult designation of suicide.[11] Obviously, it is impossible to *prove* that this is the correct explanation for the rising numbers of suicides; that would require reviewing the evidence used to assign cause of death in thousands of cases, and most of that information is probably long lost by now. But this example does remind us that even the best, most complete, most authoritative data—such as the NCHS death records—cannot speak for themselves.

Rather, numbers must be interpreted. In this case, someone at the CDC noted a rise in the number of deaths classified as suicides among African American teenagers and assumed that this must reflect a real increase in suicidal behavior. Such behavior in turn needed to be explained by identifying changes in the youths' lives that made them more suicidal. But an increase in the number of deaths classified as suicides need not reflect more acts of self-destruction; it might also reveal changes in the way officials classify deaths as suicides. Because the reported suicides were drawn from apparently authoritative official records, most commentators failed to question the rise, even though they needed convoluted explanations to account for it. Besides, scary statistics about race are common enough that many simply presume that they are correct.

Even apparently straightforward recordkeeping can prove to be extremely challenging. Consider a second example: the effort to compile the death toll from the September 11, 2001, terrorist attacks on New York's World Trade Center. Airline records made it possible to count and name the people who had been on the two jets almost immediately. But how many people died in the collapse of the buildings? No one keeps a master list of the people inside a skyscraper at any given moment. Even during the course of a normal working day, those present—employees in their offices, customers, visitors—form a large, constantly shifting population. And the airliners crashing into the buildings led many thousands of people to evacuate the towers, even as hundreds of firefighters, police, and other emergency personnel entered the structures. Moreover, when the buildings fell, the destruction was so complete that many bodies vanished without a trace.

In this case, counting the dead turned out to be very complicated. Within a few days, officials had compiled various lists of people reported missing. The names came from firms who offered lists of employees thought to have been in the buildings and from worried friends and family members who hadn't heard from people they suspected might have been in the Trade

Center. Reports continued to arrive until September 24, when the list peaked at 6,453 names.

Then the list began to get shorter. Officials began to cull duplicate names (for example, a dozen different reports had been made for the same woman, each giving different addresses or contact numbers). People who had been reported missing turned out to be alive (more than fifteen hundred foreigners initially reported missing by embassies were located). Investigations also identified some seventy fraudulent reports from people hoping to collect survivors' benefits. A handful of names were added—for example, people who had been moved to out-of-state hospitals before they died from injuries caused by the attacks. On September 11, 2002, the total had fallen to 2,801, which still included 35 to 40 people for whom there was no definitive evidence that they had—or had not—died. Even after a year of painstaking investigation, the total was not yet certain; and, in fact, it continued to change.[12]

The death toll became a subject of contention, particularly during the fall of 2001. For a few weeks, some officials continued to repeat early estimates of 5,000 or 6,000 deaths, and their rhetoric seemed to argue that these heavy losses were the justification for retaliation against the terrorists. Some even criticized the initial press stories that predicted (correctly) that the final death toll would prove to be much lower. Of course, the horror of the attack was not somehow proportionate to the numbers lost; the final death toll proved to be about half what was originally estimated, but this did not make the tragedy only half as great.

Even as some officials tried to carefully tally the casualties, others disseminated another dubious statistic about the magnitude of the catastrophe: they claimed that the World Trade

Center attack had orphaned 10,000, or even 15,000, children, many of whom would need adoption. This estimate could not pass even the most casual examination. Even if we take the peak estimate for the death toll (6,500), 15,000 orphans would have meant that each victim averaged more than two children. Moreover, if we use the conventional meaning of orphan—a minor child who has lost both parents—it is obvious that this claim was most improbable: many victims' children would have been adults; not all victims would have had children; and most married victims would have been survived by a spouse who could continue to care for their children. While thousands of family members suffered the loss of loved ones, New York's family service officials could not identify a single child of those killed in the attack who required adoption or foster care.[13] The World Trade Center attack was a terrible event, but it was still possible to circulate statistics that exaggerated the extent of the damage.

I have chosen to focus on death statistics because they seem so straightforward; it is far easier to count deaths than to measure poverty, unemployment, crime, and most of the other things officials count. Official statistics are often the most complete, the best—the most authoritative—figures we have, but that does not mean that they are perfectly accurate.

Officials have considerable advantages in collecting statistics. Compared to the research projects conducted by scientists, many official agencies have generous budgets, which allow them to pay people to collect, compile, analyze, and interpret data. Compliance with such data collection efforts may be required by law; citizens are supposed to cooperate with the census, and birth and death records are mandatory. As data go, official statistics tend to be relatively complete.

But official records are products of the political system and therefore are inevitably shaped by political considerations. Every decision to collect official information can be a focus for political debate. What information do we need? Precisely which information should we collect? How should we collect it? How should it be compiled? Which results should be made available? How should they be made available, and to whom? What sorts of resources should we devote to this process? It costs time and money to collect information, so we can assume that someone considers the collection effort to be worth the cost. In some cases, there may be widespread agreement that the information ought to be collected, that this serves some general interest; most people probably approve of keeping birth and death records, for example. People may even agree about what should be counted and how.

Very often, however, matters are more complicated, with competing interests trying to shape statistics. Chapter 1, for example, noted that ethnic minorities tend to advocate collecting census data about ethnicity in ways that maximize their groups' numbers. Or take the case of the Consumer Price Index. The CPI is widely used as a basis for calculating cost-of-living raises for union contracts and government benefits. This makes the method of calculating the CPI a matter of more than academic interest. Employers and government programs that must pay employees based on changes in the CPI favor calculations that minimize the growth of the index, whereas those whose earnings or benefits are tied to CPI increases favor calculations that maximize CPI growth. Economists who suggest ways of altering the CPI formula to reflect changes in the way people live (such as adjusting for the impact of home computers or cell phones) find their work criticized not only on intellectual grounds but also for its political implications.[14]

And, of course, officials' views of their role may vary. At one extreme, officials may see themselves as impartial professionals, collecting statistics in an unbiased manner. At the opposite extreme, officials may consider themselves active agents for some faction, such as the current political administration, and they may deliberately try to produce statistics that support its policies. (Note that this need not involve fraud or outright deception. It can simply take the form of choosing to count particular things or of publicizing particular numbers and emphasizing their importance.) Most officials probably fall between these extremes; they seek to do a competent, accurate job, yet sometimes find their work shaped by their own commitments or by political pressures from others.

THE FRAGILITY OF AUTHORITY

Authoritative statistics depend on our confidence in the institutions that collect them. Accountants, for example, certify that a firm's financial records are in good order, which assures investors that they have the information necessary to make wise investment decisions regarding that firm. The 2001–2002 revelations that Enron and other major corporations had adopted—and their accountants had approved—various dubious financial arrangements produced a major scandal that not only ruined the firms directly involved but also threatened investor confidence in the larger economy. The federal government subsequently passed a corporate reform law requiring that the chief executive officers of major corporations personally certify, under penalty of criminal sanction, that their firms' records were legitimate. In other words, because one layer of institutional protections had proven insufficient, the solution was to devise yet another layer of reassurance, in order to further guarantee the accuracy and reliability of financial recordkeeping. Confidence in authority depends on such symbols.

Such guarantees may seem to be fragile social contracts. Ordinary people cannot check or replicate the numbers produced by scientists, officials, accountants, and other authorities; the costs in time and money would be impossibly high. Instead, we rely on the professionalism of those authorities, on their pledge to meet the expectations of their clients, the law, their peers, and themselves to produce the best possible numbers. Statistics from poorer countries that lack the resources to support data collection and analysis are often little better than guesses,[15] but a rich society expects—and largely receives—high-quality statistics from its authorities. In the United States, bad statistics are scandalous. Recall the shock when, in the aftermath of the 2000 election, people began to understand that even mechanized systems of counting votes can lead to errors (for example, by failing to count ballots with hanging chads); similarly, reports of scientific fraud, officials maintaining inaccurate records, or serious accounting lapses become major news stories.

Despite our expectations, the examples in this chapter demonstrate that authoritative statistics have their limits. Data collection is never perfect; the "dark figure" of hidden, uncounted cases is always present.[16] Every analysis involves choosing what to count and how to go about counting, and those choices always shape the resulting numbers. Often, those choices reflect pressures on the authorities. In some cases, all the pressure may come from one direction, leading everyone to support the same set of choices; but in other instances, competing pressures come from those who hope, say, for a big number, while others would prefer a smaller figure. And, of course, authorities have expectations for one another: scientists use the peer review process to improve the quality of published research; accountants have generally agreed-upon standards for evaluating accounts; and so on. Inevitably, even the most authoritative statistics reflect all of these social processes. People can and do disagree about the best way to conduct the census or measure unemployment or assess the danger of bullying. Counting, even when it produces authoritative statistics, is a social process.

In short, the question to ask about any number—even those that seem most authoritative—is not "Is it true?" Rather, the most important question is "How was it produced?" If some numbers are more authoritative, it is because we have more confidence in the processes that brought them into being. But this is not to say that we should imagine that any numbers offer magical solutions to our problems.

Anyone who follows the news hears about economic recessions. In good times, commentators speculate about the risk of a recession beginning; in bad times, they wonder whether the current recession is about to end. It turns out that the authority to make these determinations, to identify when recessions begin and end, belongs to the Business Cycle Dating Committee of the federal government's National Bureau of Economic Research. This usually anonymous committee made news in the summer of 2003, when it proposed changing the criteria used to determine when a recession was ending.[1]

The committee had been using several monthly indicators of economic activity, including payroll employment (the number of people employed in payroll jobs), to identify when recessions began and ended. The formula had not included a measure of gross domestic product (GDP, the value of goods and services produced in the United States) because GDP was measured quarterly, not monthly. Because previous recessions had been marked by declines in both jobs and GDP, failing to include GDP made little difference in designating a recession's start and finish.

The recession that began in late 2001, however, broke this pattern: thanks to improved productivity, GDP began to rise in late 2002, yet payroll employment continued to decline. Because the committee's formula relied on the jobs measure, which was still falling, the official assessment was that the recession was not over, even though many observers believed that the economy had bottomed out months earlier just before GDP began to rise. Therefore, the committee decided to incorporate monthly estimates of GDP into its calculations, a step that led to a declaration that the recession had ended, although the committee acknowledged that there were continuing losses in employment.

Once again, we see the impact of people choosing what to count. Under the committee's old formula, the 2003 economy was still in a recession; under the proposed new formula, the recession would be over. The committee translates numbers—in this case, economic measures—into official labels for the state of the economy. In doing so, the committee gives those numbers importance.

Our culture depends on numbers, and therefore treats them seriously. Even when we suspect that our statistics are flawed, we realize that we can't get along without figures. The economy—and the rest of our world—is too complicated to comprehend without resorting to numbers; we need statistics to give us a basis for understanding what's happening and for making choices. Counting and measuring can help us decide what to do. When our attention is drawn to some new social problem, one of our first impulses is to quantify it, to measure its scope.

Statistics, we say, will let us "get a handle" on the problem, as though translating the problem into numbers will somehow give us the means to bring it under control or at least show us how we might achieve control. We act as though numbers have amazing powers to illuminate, to make the right choices apparent—as though they have *magical* properties.

Magical numbers, then, are figures we imagine to be accurate and authoritative, numbers that promise to make our problems understandable and therefore manageable. Magical numbers seem to transform ambiguity into certainty, to provide a basis for complicated decisions. They offer a standard against which we can assess the world. At least this is what we tell ourselves.

This suggests that we should watch for magical numbers to appear at our culture's fault lines—at those spots where conflict, uncertainty, and anxiety seem particularly intense, where we feel the need for a firmer foundation on which to base our actions. When someone draws attention to a social problem, for example, it forces us to confront claims that our society doesn't work as well as it should, that something must be done to make things better. Our culture aspires to perfectibility: we will, we insist, "leave no child behind"; we declare war on poverty, on drugs, even on cancer. Given these lofty aspirations, drawing attention to a social problem is a critique that seems to require action. Of course, some people may question whether this problem really needs attention or may disagree about the appropriate solutions. It is no wonder that such debates over social issues almost always feature statistics. Advocates often resort to numbers to bolster their claims, to make them seem more certain. Remember, our culture presumes that statistics are factual; numbers suggest that someone has measured the problem and understands its dimensions. Figures can make us feel less confused about what we ought to do.

Numbers may be unnecessary in unambiguous situations. When people's actions are governed by ritual, by the orders of those in command, or by shared moral standards, there is less room for choice, for uncertainty or anxiety. But our modern world is characterized by complexity and diversity, by competing claims and shifting standards. Uncertainty is common, and we often turn to statistics for their magical ability to clarify, to turn uncertainty into confidence, to transform fuzziness into facts. These statistics don't even need to be particularly good numbers. We seem to believe that any number is better than no number, and we sometimes seize upon whatever figures are available to reduce our confusion. The problem is that a certainty inspired by magical numbers may in fact be a poor guide for making decisions about the real world.

This chapter examines types of numbers that, at least sometimes, take on magical properties. These examples can help us understand the nature of magical numbers. We begin with a decision that confronts many families.

POSING FOR THE SWIMSUIT ISSUE

Choosing a college is an anxiety-provoking process. The cost of a four-year undergraduate education is substantial and can be counted on to rise each year. Although the same can be said about the cost of a new car, customers who walk into an auto dealership with enough money are rarely turned away, whereas most applicants to elite colleges are denied admission. This uncertainty—will I get in?—leads students to apply to more than one institution, in an attempt to ensure that they are accepted somewhere. Applicants granted admission by more than one college are able to choose among these offers.

But there are thousands of colleges out there, and the application process itself costs money. To which schools should students apply? A small industry has emerged offering guides to selecting colleges. Especially prominent is the newsmagazine *U.S. News & World Report,* which each fall publishes an annual guide for prospective students that ranks colleges based on statistical information. This issue, which sells far more copies than the magazine's regular weekly issues, is known among college admissions officers as the "swimsuit issue." The guide ranks colleges within categories ("Best National Universities–Doctoral," for instance), based on numeric scores, on seemingly objective criteria.

Now stop and ask yourself what criteria someone would use to choose a college. How about quality of education? All things considered, a high-quality education ought to be more desirable than one of lesser quality. But it is very difficult to define quality of education, let alone measure it and then rank colleges by this measure. In fact, quality of education is likely to depend on all sorts of hard-to-predict things. We might suspect that this very year we can find students at every single college in the nation who are benefiting greatly, who are getting what are, for their purposes, high-quality educations, just as we can also find students on every single campus who are having rotten experiences and getting lousy educations. But, having said that, how can we hope to convert these experiences into numbers? Recall chapter 1's discussion of the difficulties with counting the incalculable.

U.S. News resolves this dilemma by ranking colleges according to criteria that are easy to quantify. This is a common solution to this sort of problem. Colleges themselves, for example, want to promote professors who are good teachers and scholars, but it is very difficult to measure the quality of either teaching or scholarship. To make these decisions, most colleges rely heavily on criteria that produce numbers—scores on the teaching evaluations completed by students or the number of publications a professor has written—even though everyone involved acknowledges that teaching evaluation scores and numbers of publications are only loosely related to faculty quality. These imperfect measures are at least numeric and therefore allow faculty to be ranked: Professor A has better teaching evaluation scores than Professor B, and Professor X has more publications than Professor Y. Numbers seem objective; what we can express as a number often becomes the decisive measure, simply because the absence of numbers makes other criteria seem too arbitrary.

What sorts of numbers can *U.S. News* find for ranking colleges? The magazine uses a complicated formula to create its rankings, but, for our purposes, we can focus on three sorts of figures incorporated in the formula. The first concerns the qualifications of the students the colleges admit. Because the magazine looks for indicators that can be reduced to numbers that are available from every campus, two measures emerge: scores on college entrance exams, such as the Scholastic Aptitude Test (SAT), taken by prospective students; and students' high school class rank. The assumption is that colleges that admit better students—that is, students with better numbers (higher test scores and class standings)—deserve higher rankings. Once again, a qualitative concept is measured by the available quantitative standards.

The second set of measures concerns the college admission

process itself. Here it helps to think of three stages: first, prospective students apply to a college; second, the college admits some of those applicants (tells them that they are welcome to enter the college as students); and third, some of those admitted choose to attend that college. The number of students who decide to attend is important because colleges plan their budgets by assuming that they will have a certain number of students on campus in the fall. If too few students show up, the college will bring in less income than planned and will be forced to cut back; if too many students arrive, the college may not have enough professors, dorm rooms, equipment, and so on to accommodate them all. Because many students are admitted to more than one college, every college knows that some proportion of the applicants it admits will turn down its offer in favor of other institutions. Therefore, in order to be confident that enough people will show up next fall, colleges must admit more students than they can actually handle.

The three stages produce three numbers: the number of applications, the number admitted, and the number who accept admission. When we divide the second number by the first, we get the proportion of applicants who are admitted (called the *admission rate*). Dividing the third number by the second gives us the proportion of admitted students who accept the invitation to attend (called the *yield rate*). *U.S. News* uses the admission and yield rates to rank colleges. The magazine assumes that a college that admits only a small proportion of those who apply (that is, it has a low admission rate) is choosy; it takes only the best students. And, if a large proportion of those admitted choose to attend that college (that is, it has a high yield rate), those choices indicate that students view the college as desirable.

Once upon a time, admission and yield rates were internal figures, used by a college's administrators to plan. If you assume, for example, that this year's yield rate will be about the same as last year's, you have a reasonable idea of how many applicants you should admit in order to get the number of first-year students you want to arrive on campus. But now, thanks to *U.S. News* and the rest of the college admissions guidebook industry, these figures are not just public; they are also seen as a reasonable basis for comparing the quality of colleges and are part of the formulas used to calculate rankings.

Such emphasis leads colleges to try to boost their rankings by improving the numbers that *U.S. News* uses in its calculations. One way to do this is to attract more applications—even if you're already receiving plenty of good applications, increasing the total number (while accepting the same number of students) allows you to report a lower admissions rate, thereby making your college seem more selective. Similarly, one of the reasons colleges like early-decision programs is that they attract applications from students who are more likely to accept an offer of admission; increasing the number of these students raises the yield rate and thereby enhances the ranking.[2]

The third element in the *U.S. News* formula for calculating rankings is actually the most important: peer assessment, which counts for 40 percent of a college's score.[3] The magazine sends ballots to two officials at each college, who are asked to assign numeric scores to other institutions around the country. (On my campus of the University of Delaware, these ballots go to the director of public relations and the associate provost for enrollment management, who oversees the admissions process.) Right away, questions arise. What qualifies these officials to assess the quality of other colleges? Why not send ballots to people more directly involved in educating students? What possible basis can these raters have for evaluating institutions they have probably never seen? Shrewd institutions now engage in direct marketing—to these voters. In the weeks before the rating sheets arrive from *U.S. News,* the officials who will be casting ballots begin to receive advertising—glossy fact books sent out by various colleges, each extolling the virtues of its campus. Presumably an effective campaign will result in higher scores from the raters, which will lead to higher rankings.

Colleges tend to focus on these three elements in the *U.S. News* formula because they are relatively easy to change. The formula also incorporates several other factors, such as the number of faculty members, spending per student, and the graduation rate, but these are hard to alter because it would be either too expensive or too difficult to change them substantially from year to year. In contrast, encouraging more admissions and advertising the virtues of your campus to those who will cast ballots are relatively inexpensive tactics that might produce quick, favorable shifts in scores.

None of these manipulations, of course, has anything to do with the quality of education a college offers. Yet they are important, because year-to-year fluctuations in a college's ranking in the swimsuit issue can affect prospective students' application decisions. This is true even though shifts in the rankings are far more likely to reflect changes in how a college's admissions office conducts its business or how well the institution promotes itself to those who fill out the peer rating forms than anything that occurs in its classrooms.

This example reveals how magical numbers work. Magical

numbers help to resolve uncertainty. In this case, prospective students and their parents who want to make wise college decisions are confronted with a bewildering array of choices. The *U.S. News* rankings seem to offer an objective basis for making decisions: the swimsuit issue translates educational quality into a formula composed of quantifiable elements, and this formula produces numeric scores that allow us to rank colleges. Backstage, some colleges may be working to improve their rankings not by actually improving education on their campuses, but by soliciting more applications or touting themselves to the public relations officers on other campuses. This activity remains hidden, however. And those who want to place their faith in the swimsuit issue can take comfort in the belief that their decisions are rooted in nice, apparently solid statistics.

MAGIC AND ORGANIZATIONAL NUMBERS GAMES

Presumably, college rankings work their magic on individual students and their families. Many prospective students no doubt ignore these guidebooks, and, even among those who consult them, few are likely to make their college choices strictly on the basis of these rankings. The importance of the guidebooks' statistics—the degree to which they seem to exert magical power—varies among individuals. In contrast, other numbers have greater influence; they may affect many people, more or less simultaneously, within particular organizations and institutions.

While individuals sometimes turn to numbers to resolve uncertainty, most large organizations depend on statistics just to manage their day-to-day operations.[4] Organizations need numbers to assess how well things are going. Businesses need to calculate costs and sales, profits and losses, while government and other nonprofit agencies have their own budgets and schedules. Organizations generate progress reports, efficiency reports, evaluations, assessments, and all manner of other number-crunching documents. The larger the organization, the more difficult it is to keep track of everything that is happening, and the more its managers and other members will depend on numbers to summarize and clarify the complexity and to help them evaluate their own and others' performance. These figures condense reality into apparently straightforward measures; they provide the basis for the organization's decision-making. Still, the underlying process is not that different from bewildered high school students turning to college rankings: ambiguity and uncertainty encourage organizations to use statistics to simplify complexity. And, to the degree that these numbers become key to understanding and interpreting what is happening within the organization, the figures take on magical qualities.

Whenever numbers are consequential, whenever people take them seriously and use them as a basis for decisions and actions, someone has a stake in those numbers. People who make decisions on the basis of statistics provided by others need to believe that those figures are correct, accurate, and valid—and they may try to ensure that they're given good data. In turn, the people who are affected by those decisions prefer numbers that lead to favorable outcomes; statistics that encourage your boss to increase your budget are clearly preferable to figures that might cause your boss to fire you. People care about numbers, and the more magical the number—the more it is treated as significant and meaningful, as the basis for decision-making—the more they are likely to care. And, since all numbers are produced by someone counting something, there are sure to be efforts to influence the production of—the counting that leads to—magical numbers. We have already seen one such example: the various attempts by colleges to raise their rankings in the *U.S. News* swimsuit issue. Analogous moves occur in most organizations.

Organizational numbers take two principal forms: some are for internal use, while others are intended for external purposes. Internally, subordinates such as managers of particular departments might be required to report figures on expenditures or productivity to their bosses, who use these numbers to decide which units deserve more support or need closer supervision. Inevitably, complexity—all the factors that affect everything that is happening within the organization—gets condensed into a few numeric measures. But what is measured? When is it measured? How is it measured? The answers to such questions reflect choices about what counts within that organization. When a boss requires subordinates to report certain numbers, the assumption is that those figures can provide a picture of what's important.

Requirements to report statistics to others within the organization set the stage for bureaucratic "numbers games." Obviously, a magical number that works in one's favor is a good number; subordinates have every reason to cooperate in producing such statistics. But if numbers imply that a unit has problems, it might be possible to minimize their impact. A canny subordinate might be able to manipulate the figures in a report in order to convey the best possible impression, perhaps even to suggest that this unit is doing a particularly good job, that it is more efficient, more productive, more deserving of reward than rival units. Alternatively, when the requested figures can't be massaged to provide a favorable picture, an experienced subordinate might argue that the measures are imperfect, that they fail to assess what is really important or to recognize what the unit does well, that these data are meaningless, and that alternative measures are in order.

In turn, shrewd supervisors will be aware of their subordinates' interest in putting the best face on things, and they will try to ensure that the numbers they receive are accurate. In cases when suspect numbers are reported, supervisors might demand additional reports using new measures, or they might insist on specific, standardized methods of measuring and reporting. These new demands then invite subordinates to consider how they might also turn these new numbers to advantage. When supervisors fail to exert such control, the organization can be plagued by false figures. For example, the former Soviet Union's statistics on agricultural production—generated by subordinates more frightened by the penalties for reporting poor harvests than by concern that their false reports might be discovered—stand as a monument to this sort of internal deception.[5]

Other numbers have external audiences; they are seen—and treated as meaningful—by people outside the organization. Investors, for example, use the figures in corporate financial reports to decide whether firms are attractive investments. When an organization is aware that outsiders will be examining the numbers it produces, its members may work to shape the numbers in order to convey the desired impression to that audience. Once again, a "numbers game" is being played, only now not all the players are within the organization. Thus, some critics argue that because contemporary investors pay particular attention to corporate quarterly earnings—"the Number"—corporations now favor business policies and accounting practices that can generate favorable earnings that match or exceed market expectations, even if different actions might be in the firm's (and investors') long-run interest.[6] Similarly, police departments sometimes classify crimes in ways that minimize the crime rates in their cities, thereby implying that the police are doing an effective job.[7] Whenever outsiders are known to use magical numbers to assess organizational performance, the organization has opportunities to affect that assessment. (Remember those colleges trying to enhance their guidebook rankings.)

In turn, knowing that an organization may manipulate its statistics, outsiders can try to gain a measure of control over the numbers. They might insist that the organization report certain information in certain ways. For example, when the FBI asks police departments to fill out the *Uniform Crime Report* forms that serve as the basis for calculating crime rates, the bureau gives detailed instructions for what to count and how to count it. Similarly, the U.S. Securities and Exchange Commission specifies a general format for corporate financial reporting. These are efforts to make reports from different organizations comparable. The outsiders may even try to establish and enforce penalties for those who disseminate incorrect numbers. Such measures can discourage deceptive reporting, but, as the Enron scandal reminds us, they cannot ensure that the reported figures will be accurate.[8]

The point is that organizations need statistics to operate, both to provide a basis for their internal decisions and as a means of summarizing their activities to outsiders. But to the degree that people either inside or outside the organization take those figures seriously and use them as a basis for decisions—that is, the more magical the numbers are—the more the organization's members have a stake in shaping the statistics to match their own interests. It would be naive to imagine that statistics reported by organizations simply mirror reality, that they reflect the simple, whole truth. We must acknowledge that there are trade-offs. Organizational numbers always condense complexity, which has both benefits and costs: such numbers allow us to summarize, to clarify, to grasp the big picture; but these summaries inevitably simplify, as people choose what to count and how to count it. The more consequential (magical) the numbers are, the more likely people are to think carefully about those choices and work to make the numbers convey their side of the story, and the less confidence we can have in the figures as a straightforward reflection of reality.

This is the paradox of magical numbers: we need them, and we need to be able to trust them; yet the greater our need, the more likely that the figures will be distorted, and the more care we must take when examining them. Before we can rely on statistics, we need to ask who counted what, and how and why they counted it—because, as our next example shows, when magical numbers become the focus of widespread attention, the potential for confusion is very great.

JUDGING SCHOOLS

Anxiety about the quality of American education grew to remarkable levels during the last decades of the twentieth century. This might seem curious. After all, Americans' average years of schooling increased dramatically throughout the century. In

1900, only about 6 percent of American seventeen-year-olds graduated from high school.[9] By the century's end, most Americans were continuing their education beyond high school, and about a third of those in recent age cohorts completed bachelor's degrees. The United States now has one of the largest percentages of highly educated citizens in the world.[10] Other statistics, however, were troubling. Studies found that Americans students often scored less well on comparative tests than students in other countries, particularly in math and science, subjects in which cultural differences should have only a minimal impact (since the answers are either right or wrong). This comparison indicated that American students weren't learning as much or as well as their counterparts elsewhere. And scores on the SAT, the principal college admissions test, dropped from the mid-1960s through about 1980, which suggested that the performance of American students might actually be getting worse. (Since 1980, SAT math scores have largely recovered, although verbal scores have remained low.)[11]

This evidence raised doubts about the quality of American education and student accomplishment, and critics expressed concerns about what this might mean for the country's future. Perhaps it was once possible to drop out of school and still make a reasonable living, but the modern job market requires more education—it offers fewer jobs that demand strong backs and more that need nimble brains. Today's drop-out seems to be risking a lifetime of marginal poverty. Moreover, a country that fails to maximize its citizens' education risks falling behind other nations that do a better job of educating their young. Nor, these critics warned, should Americans find comfort in the higher rates of school completion; graduating larger numbers of less able students is simply proof that schools have abandoned academic standards. These critics offered a nostalgic vision of the educational past: in the good old days, students worked hard; they really learned their lessons; they were dedicated, determined. But these kids today! They don't know things, they don't care, they don't read, they watch television, and their music—if you can call it music. . . . Inevitably, the critics began to sound like their parents.

Nostalgia offers a faulty lens for viewing change. Each generation's educational critics tend to be people who themselves did pretty well in school, at least well enough to acquire the credentials to become critics. They remember themselves and their friends as being fairly good students, and they often forget their classmates who did less well or who may have left school. Contrasting the critics' memories with today's students does not necessarily compare apples with apples. Even changes in standardized test scores may prove tricky to evaluate. If we assume that, in general, the more able students stay in school the longest, then, as the share of young people who remain in high school or enter college increases, the average abilities of high school graduates or college students might decline because more lower-performing students are continuing to pursue education. Thus, measuring educational achievement across time may well compare scores from rather different populations of students.

Still, criticizing schools appeals to all sorts of critics. Conservatives can blame poor performance on schools having drifted away from a traditional academic curriculum and strict discipline, and they call for a return to these fundamental principles. Liberals can argue that schools are failing to reach students who are somehow disadvantaged and that the curriculum needs to be modified to educate those most vulnerable students. Whatever a critic's particular agenda, most agree that something must be done, although the critics probably won't agree on just what that something should be. And a society that preaches perfectionism—"we will leave no child behind"—seems particularly likely to see schools as falling short and criticisms of education as well founded.

Recently, this anxiety about education has led to the widespread adoption of standardized educational testing as a means of holding schools accountable. The states and the federal government require that all public school students be given standardized tests and that the results—particularly the average scores at different schools—be made public. These tests have various consequences. For individual students, poor test scores may lead to mandatory summer school to help them catch up; in some school districts, students who complete the required courses but who cannot achieve some minimum test scores may receive a lower grade of high school diploma than their higher-scoring classmates. Teachers also face consequences. Some advocate that teachers whose students perform better on the tests should receive larger "merit" salary raises than colleagues whose students do not do as well. In addition, schools are singled out. Newspapers report the test results by school, implying that some schools are doing a better job than others; in some states, schools that show unusually large improvements in test scores receive awards. The implications reverberate outside education: realtors find that being located in a high-scoring school district has become a selling point for houses. The test scores, in short, have become an especially vivid example of magical numbers.

For educational testing to have serious consequences for students, teachers, and schools, we must make certain assumptions about what the tests measure. Most obviously, we must assume that the tests provide a valid measure of students' learning and abilities, that students who receive higher math scores actually have learned more math. But we must also assume that the teaching that occurs in schoolrooms is the key to this learning. At first, this might seem beyond dispute—"Isn't learning exactly why we send students to school—and isn't teaching exactly what schools are supposed to do?"

But note the familiar role of social class in schooling: in general, upper-middle-class (disproportionately white) students tend to do better in school than lower-class (disproportionately black or Latino) students. The causes for this pattern are hotly debated. Various explanations emphasize differences in the students (for instance, arguments that intelligence is determined partly by genetics), differences in the students' social circumstances (for example, whether family, friends, and other people in the students' lives value and support education), and differences in schooling (such as whether upper-middle-class children attend schools with better teachers, smaller classes, nicer facilities, and a variety of other advantages). Different explanations carry varying implications for testing policies. Thus, if we assume that what happens in school is the principal factor in determining how much students learn, then test scores might be a good index of school performance. But if we assume that students' social circumstances have powerful effects on shaping learning, then test scores may ultimately measure little more than the students' social class.

This is one reason debates over testing policies have become so acrimonious. Advocates of testing argue that schools and teachers ought to be doing a much better job and that they must be held accountable by using students' test scores as the measure of the educators' performance. Presumably, if educators do the job they are paid to do, their students will pass the tests. If students at some schools perform poorly on the tests, they can be required to take summer school, they may not qualify for academic diplomas, their teachers should receive lower merit raises, and so on. In short, the scores will have serious consequences.

As these consequences have become apparent, critics of testing have become more vocal. Not surprisingly, many teachers and principals oppose testing systems that penalize educators for students' poor performance. Teachers' unions argue that teachers are being blamed for the social circumstances of their students: "Of course children who come from upper-middle-class homes filled with books, who have two educated parents who emphasize the importance of education, and who benefit from other advantages do well in school. Lower-class children who lack those advantages can be expected to have more trouble learning, and we should not blame the teachers for things they can't control." Other critics argue that even good test scores may be an illusion, because high-stakes testing will lead schools to "teach the test," that is, to drill their students in the sorts of questions that appear on the tests, while ignoring other, perhaps more important, forms of learning. Such critiques are precisely the sorts of reactions we ought to expect from those whose performance is being assessed when large institutions adopt magical numbers: teachers (who are being evaluated by their students' scores) argue that tests cannot possibly accurately measure whether teachers are doing a good job, while nonteachers suspect that teachers may alter their instruction in ways that maximize their students' scores but diminish the actual quality of the teaching. There are even reports of teachers helping students cheat in order to improve their scores.[12]

We also encounter other problems with the way scores are put to use. For example, some states award special recognition to schools that show marked improvement in year-to-year test scores, a practice that is probably misguided. Research has shown that the schools with substantial year-to-year shifts in scores tend to have fewer students,[13] which suggests that the numbers taken to measure excellence in teaching may be nothing more than statistical artifacts. Imagine a small elementary school with a single classroom for each grade. The year-to-year scores in such a school are relatively volatile; if this year's class contains just a couple of very good students, this year's third-graders may score markedly higher than last year's class filled with ordinary students, even if the teacher taught exactly the same lessons both years. Such year-to-year variation is less likely in a larger school with, say, five rooms of third-graders; there, a couple of bright students will have less effect on the school's performance, and test scores are likely to remain fairly stable. Even if students score randomly on tests, small schools are much more likely to have their scores increase—and decrease—from year to year than large schools. But, of course, when test scores are treated as magical numbers—*the* definitive measure of how well schools and teachers and students are doing—the possibility that chance might play a role in shaping scores disappears from policy discussions.

Educational testing, with its promise of bringing schools under control, is in vogue and promises to remain there for a while—at least until this policy's limitations become more apparent. It offers a clear example of the power of magical numbers, and it ought to serve as a caution for other would-be numeric reformers.

RACIAL PROFILING

Another contentious issue in recent years has been the practice of racial profiling by police. We need to begin by recognizing that different people use the term *racial profiling* to refer to very different things. Here, I will restrict my discussion to claims about police stopping cars partly on the basis of the driver's race. Many police officers argue, and the courts have generally agreed, that race may sometimes be considered a relevant characteristic—not the sole reason, but one of several—in deciding to stop a car. Suppose, for example, that police have reason to believe that drugs are being transported along a particular route, in particular sorts of vehicles, by couriers for an African American criminal network; under these circumstances, police might decide to stop a suspicious vehicle in part because its driver is black. This is how defenders of racial profiling tend to describe the policy.

In contrast, critics of racial profiling talk about being pulled over for "DWB" ("driving while black"). Many African Americans believe that they are far more likely than white drivers to be stopped by police, because police suspect that blacks are more likely to be involved in criminal activities. In such cases, a driver's race may be the sole basis for stopping a vehicle.[14] In this view, racial profiling is a racist practice. Some critics argue that race should never be a consideration in stopping a vehicle.

Almost as soon as racial profiling emerged as a visible political issue, people began calling for the collection of statistics that could determine, once and for all, the existence and extent of the practice. That is, they demanded a magical number, a measure of racial profiling. Collecting statistics has become a popular compromise measure in contemporary politics; for instance, the first federal law concerning hate crimes required the FBI to begin counting hate crimes in order to measure the scope of the problem. Such compromises imply that statistics can magically resolve disputes. Statistics are viewed as factual, as offering a clear, unbiased portrait of police practices, hate crimes, or whatever else is at issue. It is difficult to oppose collecting such statistics because data collection is assumed to be nothing more than determining the facts. Besides, the participants in a debate may all believe that the statistics will support their position: in the case of racial profiling, the police may anticipate that such statistics will reveal that they behave responsibly, whereas their critics may assume that the numbers will expose discriminatory practices.

The problem is that measuring racial profiling is likely to be much trickier than we might think.[15] The simplest studies of racial profiling compare the race of drivers stopped to the racial composition of the area's population. Suppose that 20 percent of drivers stopped by a town's traffic officers are black. Before we can interpret that finding, we need to know something about the population of drivers on the road. Are 10 percent of the area's drivers black (which would suggest that African Americans are stopped far more often than might be expected)? Are 20 percent of the drivers black (which would suggest that the proportion of African Americans stopped is about what we would expect)? Or are 30 percent of the area's drivers black (which would suggest that African Americans are stopped less often than other drivers)? Making such comparisons is simpler in theory than in practice, however.

The key issue is how to identify the population of drivers that should be used as the basis for comparison. One criminologist calls this problem "searching for the denominator."[16] The easiest basis for comparison is the racial composition of a town's population (available from census statistics). But notice that not everyone in a town's population drives; presumably, we ought to adjust our population estimate by trying to determine the racial composition of the town's licensed drivers. But not all licensed drivers drive the same number of miles—and we might assume that the more one drives, the greater the risk of being stopped by the police.

In addition, if some roads are driven mostly by locals, the drivers presumably reflect the community's population. But other roads, such as interstate highways, carry a large proportion of drivers from elsewhere, who will not reflect the local population. The driving population probably changes from daytime to nighttime, and weekday to weekend, and we should not be surprised to find that police decisions to stop drivers may depend on time of day. For example, officers might be more likely to stop someone for reckless driving late at night, on the grounds that late-night drivers might be intoxicated. In short, getting people to agree to gather data on the racial distribution of drivers who get stopped by police is only part of the problem; we also need to agree on a basis for comparison.

A somewhat more sophisticated approach is to try to measure the race of traffic violators. In one early study, researchers drove at the speed limit down a stretch of interstate highway in Maryland and observed all the cars that passed them (which had to be speeding and therefore were theoretically eligible to be stopped by the state troopers who patrolled the road). The study found that 18 percent of the speeding drivers appeared to be black, whereas 28 percent of the drivers stopped by the Maryland state police were black.

While the results of this study were certainly suggestive, it is not difficult to identify its flaws. Everyday experience tells us that a substantial proportion of drivers exceed the speed limit, but that police ordinarily will not stop a driver going slightly— say, up to ten miles per hour—above the limit. Therefore, a study that treats all drivers who exceed the limit as eligible to be stopped may not have identified the relevant population. If, for example, whites are relatively more likely to drive just a few miles above the limit, while blacks tend to drive faster than that, then the proportion of those driving fast enough to attract police attention who are black might be greater than the percentage of African Americans among those drivers who exceed the speed limit.

All manner of other complexities suggest themselves. Speeding in and of itself may not be what leads police to stop cars. Perhaps they are equally—or more—interested in reckless driving. Perhaps they focus on older cars, which might be more likely to have visibly faulty equipment. If African Americans drive older cars, or more often drive recklessly, this might help account for them being stopped more often. Or perhaps there are demographic differences between drivers of different races. We know that young drivers get into more accidents. If the population of black drivers contains a larger proportion of young drivers, we might expect them to attract a disproportionate amount of attention from the authorities.

The point is not that any of these explanations is necessarily true. Rather, it is that using the race of drivers who pass a researcher's car that is moving at the speed limit is an imperfect way to identify drivers whom police might decide to stop. The Maryland study's statistical findings are suggestive, but they are hardly ironclad proof of the extent of racial profiling.

In short, measuring racial profiling is not the simple, straightforward matter that it might seem. However data on racial profiling are collected, some will argue that the resulting statistics are illegitimate. The call to gather data seems based on the belief that these statistics will be generally accepted as magical numbers, but it is unlikely that everyone will grant these figures that sort of authority.

These problems do not necessarily mean, however, that data collection wouldn't be worthwhile. We might suspect that police departments that collect data on the race of the drivers stopped by their officers might find the information useful. The discovery, for example, that some officers—or even one particular officer—stop far larger percentages of African American drivers than other officers patrolling the same streets would seem to raise legitimate issues. The officers in question might be asked to explain why their pattern of stops differs from those of their colleagues. Even the knowledge that information is being collected, that a record of one's performance will be reviewed, may encourage police officers to evaluate their own actions, to make sure that their traffic stops are appropriate and justifiable. (Some critics warn of another outcome: officers manipulating their records to obscure evidence of racially based actions. Once more, we see how an organization's decision to keep statistical records might lead its members to try and shape the resulting numbers.)

Collecting and examining data on the race of drivers stopped may well lead to desirable outcomes. But such data should not be understood as somehow providing a precise, perfect measure of the extent of racial profiling. Every attempt to measure racial profiling will require making choices, choices that someone may question. The resulting numbers may have their uses, but they also will have their flaws, and people might have reason to question their magical status.

THE USES OF MAGIC

The examples in this chapter illustrate a dilemma. We live in a complicated world, and we need statistics to help make the complexity understandable. We tend, then, to seize upon whatever numbers are available, to treat them as factual, accurate distillations of reality—in other words, we treat them as if they have a magical power to summarize and clarify, to provide a firm basis for decisions. But as soon as people become aware that someone has begun to treat a number as magical, the "number games" begin; folks try to manipulate the number so that the magic can work in their favor.

Once we understand this process, we should appreciate two reasons why we need to handle magical numbers with special care. The first, of course, is that we must consider the choices that underpin these statistics. People distill complexity into simplicity by making choices, by highlighting some features and dropping others from consideration. Such choices are both inevitable and consequential. Yet once we are given a number, we often forget to consider how those choices shaped the outcome. Remembering this process is essential if we are to avoid being taken in by magical numbers. The second concern is that we need to be especially alert to the possibility that people with a stake in the outcome may have manipulated these figures. The more magical the number, the more likely it is that someone affected by it will try to play a numbers game, and the more important it is to question how and why people created the figure and how its magical status affects the ways people count.

I t is no trick to spot controversies about statistics. Arguments over numbers make the news. Have Hispanics become the nation's largest ethnic minority? Should federal guidelines for acceptable levels of arsenic in drinking water be modified? Is hormone replacement therapy beneficial or dangerous? Such questions highlight debates about data.

The widespread assumption that statistics can reduce complexity to summaries of simple facts is more than just a way of attributing magical power to numbers. It is also a way to win arguments. In debates over social and political questions, people sometimes present statistics as though they are rhetorical trump cards, facts that can overwhelm any opposition. Because figures are considered such powerful evidence, they often cannot be ignored but must be challenged, either with questions about their accuracy or with rival numbers. As a result, people who introduce statistics in order to win debates may find themselves arguing about numbers.

Not all statistics inspire strong opposition. Some advocates address matters of consensus. Child pornography, say, has few defenders. Statistical claims about such topics of consensus can get a free ride; often, no one inspects them closely. But other social issues become matters of bitter debate because they invoke competing ideologies or interests. And, where there is a clear basis for opposition, statistics offered by one side regularly draw critiques from the other.

These statistical controversies—what I've called *stat wars*—take different forms.[1] The simplest disputes concern the accuracy of a single number. A figure is brought to people's attention, only to have its accuracy challenged for some reason ("is that really the correct number of alcohol-related traffic deaths?"). Often, the issue is whether the people counting have done a careful and complete job, whether their definitions or methods might have led to a number that is too high or too low. In some cases, as when statistics are merely estimates, the number can be easily called into question. It is common for a lone number to be advanced—and challenged—because it serves as a kind of shorthand proof for some claim ("this problem needs to be treated seriously, as evidenced by our large estimate for the number of cases"). To the degree that a number is central to the argument, opponents will challenge that figure, either by pointing to reasons to doubt the number or by countering the original estimate with one of their own.

Debates over single numbers tend to occur early in the history of public issues, when people are trying to draw attention to a social problem, before they have had time to collect a lot of information about the topic. One sign that an issue has matured is a proliferation of statistics: more people start counting more of the problem's elements in more ways. A body of research studies may emerge; some topics may generate hundreds or thousands of numeric findings, with advocates sifting through them in a search for statistics that seem rhetorically powerful. As the pool of available statistics expands, so do opportunities to locate figures that one can use to support different stances. Advocates who search a sufficiently large pool of data can probably come up with evidence to support whatever position they favor, but their opponents are also likely to find figures that they can use to make the opposite case. Soon, statistics become weapons, rhetorical grenades lobbed at the opponents' positions.

Those who already favor a particular position in one of these debates find comfort in their side's numbers, while the opposition's figures strike them as dubious, perhaps even fraudulent. Those of us who don't have a stake in an issue—the uncommitted public is often the target audience for competing numeric claims—can become frustrated by the flow of apparently contradictory numbers. "Just tell us," we snarl, "which chemicals cause cancer." We don't want a bunch of contradictory statistics—we want the simple facts.

But facts are socially constructed. What we recognize as facts are products of people's efforts to make sense of the world, to assemble enough evidence to support a general agreement that something is true. I am not arguing that there is no real world against which we can check our facts—there is. We all know that when we hold a rock in front of us and let go, it will fall down. Insisting that it will remain suspended in space won't make that happen. Still, what knowledge is considered factual varies from time to time and place to place: for example, the most authoritative explanations for the causes of disease vary from one society to the next and across historical periods.

What we deem factual depends on a combination of evidence and consensus. Evidence matters; claims that germs might cause disease received a huge boost when microscopes let people see microbes. But consensus is also necessary; it took time and considerable research before medical opinion came to a general agreement about the value of the germ theory. Over time, the boundaries of consensus expand, although areas of dispute may remain. When we grumble that news stories about what is or isn't a cancer threat seem to change from week to week, we are complaining about a lack of consensus—which, in turn, probably reflects available evidence that is weak or deemed inconsistent.

There is an important point here. Debates about what is true tend to polarize around two weak positions. At one pole are the relativists, those postmodern theoreticians who imply that reality is up for grabs, that we can't really know anything, that we should be open to every alternative perspective and suspicious of any purported authority. The extreme version of this position justifies all manner of paranormal beliefs, conspiracy theories, and other ideas grounded in little or no evidence. The other pole is the realm of the absolutists, who insist that facts are facts and who have no patience with challenges to authoritative knowledge.

This book argues for a position somewhere between these extremes. We are social beings. Everything we know about the world, every number and, for that matter, every word we use while thinking, is shaped by our social life. Anyone who has seen an infant grow into a child knows that we all had to learn language—and, in the process, we also learned our culture's way of dividing the world into categories. The great contribution of classical anthropology was to demonstrate cultural diversity, the many different ways people could make sense of their worlds. Every culture has ideas about why people get sick, expectations for how modestly young women ought to behave, and so on—and every culture believes that its ideas and expectations are right and true. To understand our world, we must recognize that all knowledge is filtered through peoples' cultures. In short, there has to be a place for relativism.

On the other hand, science offers a particularly useful standard for evaluating some sorts of knowledge about the world. Science is a process by which ideas are tested in ways that might disprove them; ideas that survive these tests are considered more likely to be true. Over time, this process produces knowledge in which we have great confidence. This process is not perfectly smooth: findings may be initially accepted but later withdrawn when further tests call them into question; ideas may be ignored or rejected but later achieve acceptance; and so on. But these irregularities in assembling scientific knowledge should not be taken as evidence that the process doesn't work over the long run.

I wrote the first draft of this paragraph on a computer, a machine that is the product of centuries of gradually increasing scientific knowledge. I have great confidence that the machine will work, even though I must confess that I have only a primitive understanding of the scientific principles by which it operates. Yet it would be silly for me to argue that the science behind that computer was essentially arbitrary, just one of many ways of thinking about the world, no better or worse than any other. The computer works. Vaccinations work. Scientific knowledge is not just one view among other, equally valid perspectives. We can have great confidence in well-established scientific findings. In short, there has to be a place for authority grounded in evidence.

Still, science cannot answer all questions. It can tell us how and why some people get sick (though it cannot, at this point, explain all illness). But it cannot tell us how modestly young women ought to behave; that is not a topic subject to scientific evaluation. The limitations of science pose a problem in our culture, precisely because we have such high expectations for science. When we fall ill, we expect that a physician will be able to diagnose and treat what's wrong, and we become frustrated when this doesn't happen. We even use research documenting social patterns or assessing risks to recommend ways to behave. Our society treats data—statistics—as offering, if not complete answers, at least information relevant to devising the answers for many kinds of questions, including many that do not necessarily fall within the purview of science.

When confronted with statistics, we need to avoid the poles of both extreme relativism and extreme absolutism. We need to remember that statistics are social products and that the process by which they are created inevitably shapes the resulting numbers. But we must also appreciate that science offers ways of weighing the evidence, of assessing the accuracy of figures. These concerns become particularly important when statistics become the subject of disagreements.

Junk science is a term, currently in vogue, used to dismiss findings as products of dubious research. Because science is considered a source of authoritative knowledge in our culture, many people call themselves scientists as a way of legitimizing their views. Billing some set of claims as "scientific" is a modern way of claiming legitimacy and authority. Thus, some religious opponents of teaching evolution argue that they represent "creation science," and they insist that the Biblical account of creation ought to have equal footing with the explanations advanced by physical and biological scientists for the origins of the universe, the Earth, and human life. Similarly, all manner of parapsychologists, psychic healers, and perpetual-motion advocates label their views "scientific."[2]

But science is more than a name; it is an orientation toward evidence. Scientists must be prepared to test their ideas, and it must be possible for the tests to disconfirm those ideas. This is not quite the simple, pure process of hypothesis testing that junior high school textbooks describe. Scientists are people, and they may get caught up in their ideas, sometimes making excuses when those ideas fail in tests—something wasn't right with the test conditions, further tests are needed, and so on. We can point to the foibles of scientists who cling to their ideas in the face of challenging, even disconfirming evidence; focusing on such behavior allows us to draw a portrait of science that emphasizes its warts and flaws.[3] Some relativist critics argue that disagreements within science render it just one more viewpoint, no truer than any other. Perhaps one way out of this tangle is to recognize science as an ideal, but to acknowledge that individual scientists may fall short of this ideal.

Nevertheless, over time, as the available evidence grows, science accumulates a body of knowledge in which we have great confidence, based on the reliability with which its predictions are confirmed. This scientific progress depends on a community that demands rigorous, continual self-examination, subjecting ideas to tests that can determine whether the evidence supports the ideas. Because every test has weaknesses, it is the cumulative application of multiple tests that provides the foundation for science's eventual acceptance of only those ideas that hold up under the most vigorous examination.

Single studies, then, can't do the job. Absolutely every study—every test, every piece of research—has limitations and flaws in its methods that make it a target for legitimate criticism. Studies should be replicated, and they should also inspire further research that uses different methods (with, presumably, different limitations and flaws). When replication and differing methodologies confirm the same result, confidence in that finding grows. The results of a lone study, particularly if the research raises serious methodological concerns, should not, in most scientists' view, be treated as authoritative. Only time and further research can sort out the erroneous findings from the more reliable.

Unfortunately, news coverage of scientific research tends to be less patient than the scientific community.[4] The news media favor stories that seem novel, unexpected, dramatic. The most compelling scientific news story is about a sudden breakthrough, not a replication or a confirmation of an earlier finding using a different research design. Thus, the press prefers reporting exactly those research results that lack strong substantiation. A single study with a disturbing finding makes good news, and the media coverage is likely to downplay or even ignore the research's methodological limitations. As a consequence, we must approach press reports of research results with caution. This is particularly true given the efforts by some prestigious journals to promote their visibility by issuing press releases that highlight the most dramatic findings in articles they publish (as discussed in chapter 4).

The pejorative label "junk science" typically implies a methodological critique, an argument that the research was designed or the data collected in ways that make it impossible to have confidence in the results. Often, it also implies that the research was guided by a particular agenda, shaping the findings to support a specific position. The original usage of the term *junk science* was to characterize expert witnesses' testimony in trials.[5] Lawyers ask expert witnesses to testify in hopes that their expertise will persuade judges and juries that particular arguments are factually true, supported by scientific research. When an expert witness is invited to testify (and is paid) by one side in a trial, it is reasonable to wonder whether that testimony will be complete, even-handed, and actually representative of scientific consensus.

Consider, for example, the issue of "toxic" breast implants.[6] In the late 1980s and early 1990s, the health risks of breast implants became a subject of considerable public concern: the Food and Drug Administration banned silicone-filled implants; the issue received extensive media coverage; and a multibillion-dollar class-action lawsuit was filed. Critics of the implants were bolstered by various medical and scientific experts who presented evidence that a number of women who had implants experienced certain diseases. We see a familiar line of reasoning here: someone falls ill, tries to understand what caused the illness, recalls some experience (such as having breast implants), and concludes that the experience must have caused the illness. The logic may seem perfectly compelling to the individual, but it cannot be considered scientific proof.

Science demands, among other things, epidemiological support. For example, we know that some people get sick, so we should expect some level of sickness among women who have breast implants simply because they are people. Therefore, the key question is whether women with breast implants are any more likely to fall ill than other, similar women who have not had implants. (Recall chapter 3's discussion of risk: the usual standard for such comparisons is that the rate of illness should be at least 200 percent greater among women with breast implants than in the control group before we can conclude that implants probably cause disease.) In general, epidemiological studies did not show such higher rates of disease among women with implants. This evidence should have been viewed as a very serious challenge to claims that implants were harmful, but critics of implants won the public relations battle (and many of the court cases), partly because the results of the epidemiological studies did not become known until very late in the issue's history.

One problem with the notion of junk science is that the term has become politically loaded: conservatives often use it to dismiss claims by environmentalists, consumer advocates, and other activists warning about dangers in contemporary society.[7] In response, liberal critics argue that "the concept of junk science serves as a convenient way of reconciling . . . pro-corporate bias with pretensions of scientific superiority."[8] Each side argues that scientists on the other side are biased and cannot be trusted to design legitimate research. It is difficult for nonspecialists to assess these claims and counterclaims, if only because the differences in research findings may derive from competing assumptions, definitions, or methodological choices. For example, scientists working with environmentalists may define infrequent exposure to a very low concentration of a radioactive substance as a dangerous health risk, whereas scientists working for industry may argue that more frequent exposure to higher concentrations of the same substance does not pose an unacceptable risk.[9] Both sides may insist that theirs is the scientifically sound position, that their method of assessing risk is appropriate—leaving nonscientists frustrated by the need to weigh the claims of dueling experts.

Although its links to particular ideological positions may make it impossible to rehabilitate the term *junk science,* a useful idea is lurking in this debate. Every piece of research contains limitations; researchers inevitably choose specific definitions, measures, designs, and analytic techniques. These choices are consequential; they shape every study's results. We can never have as much confidence in the results of any single study as we can in a body of research, in which the various researchers' choices help cancel out one another's limitations. Our confidence that smoking causes lung cancer is not founded on any single study, but on a large body of studies using different methods that—overall—link smoking with cancer. To be sure, some researchers have biases that lead them to design research in ways that may foster the results they favor; don't forget that the Tobacco Institute once sponsored research intended to generate results suggesting that smoking was not especially harmful. But the real problem with much of what is called junk science is not so much the researchers' motives or politics as it is the advocates' tendency to proclaim one or two preliminary studies as definitive. In such cases, the process of assembling scientific data gets short-circuited by political concerns.

Debates over junk science have another notable feature. They tend to involve disagreements about notions of trade-offs and risks (raised in chapters 1 and 3)—will this chemical (medical procedure, hydroelectric project) cause unacceptable harm? Reasonable people might disagree about all sorts of issues here. How should we measure prospective harm? How should we weigh the harms (or costs) against the projected benefits (and how should we measure those)? While advocates may try to characterize such debates as contests between good and evil, the evaluation of scientific evidence is rarely so straightforward.

SPINNING AND CHERRY-PICKING

Debates over social statistics rarely begin as disputes about a number. Rather, they almost always start as disagreements about the importance of a social issue or the solution to a social problem, with advocates proceeding to introduce numbers as ammunition to reinforce one position or another. Recent political discourse refers to *spinning,* the practice of offering the media an interpretation of events that coincides with one's own viewpoint, in hopes that the media will repeat—and possibly even endorse—that viewpoint.[10] Numbers can be subjects of spinning.

Consider the conflicting interpretations offered when officials announced that the 2000 census revealed that a growing proportion—about one-quarter—of households were composed of lone individuals.[11] For conservative, pro-family advocates, this statistic was further evidence of the decline of the traditional American family, of the need for social policies to promote families. But other, more liberal commentators interpreted the increase in single-person households in more positive terms: growing affluence and improved health meant that young people could afford to set up independent living arrangements, that individuals could end unsatisfactory marriages, and that the elderly could maintain their own households. Thus, one could read census statistics documenting the growth in single-person households as revealing either societal decay or improved living circumstances. Note that no one disputed the statistic's accuracy; people can acknowledge that a number is basically correct without necessarily agreeing about what it means. The glass can be seen as half-full or half-empty—it just depends on the spin.

The existence of well-articulated, competing ideologies encourages spinning. We are accustomed to hearing competing interpretations from Democrats and Republicans, or conservatives and liberals, and statistics offer opportunities for spinning by these rivals. Thus, reports that a growing proportion of young Americans are overweight invite critiques from the left, targeting the food industry's campaigns to promote high-calorie products, and from the right, noting the obesity-enhancing effects of federal school lunch programs.[12] In most cases, the arguments chosen, the factors blamed for the problem, and the nature of the solutions proposed are predictable to anyone familiar with the ideologies.

The more figures available, the more opportunities for spinning. For example, the federal government collects extensive data regarding social problems such as drug use. Surveys of high school seniors, known as Monitoring the Future (MTF), provide one of the standard means for tracking drug use. Administered during most years, the MTF surveys generate statistics on seniors' self-reported use of different drugs over various periods of time. For example, we can learn that, in 2000, 21.6 percent of high school seniors reported smoking marijuana, and 50 percent reported drinking alcohol during the previous thirty days.[13] What should we make of these numbers? Are things getting better or worse? It depends on which years and which drugs are used for comparison. For example, in 1990—ten years earlier—14 percent of seniors reported smoking marijuana, so marijuana smoking was 50 percent higher in 2000; however, during the same period, drinking alcohol declined, from 57.1 percent to 50 percent. Nor are the trends all that steady; almost every MTF report offers more than enough numbers to allow someone who picks figures carefully to argue, based on statistics, that teen drug use has either increased or decreased during a particular period.

Such arguments are one form of *cherry-picking* (sometimes called *data dredging*)—that is, selecting statistics that support a particular thesis and drawing attention to those numbers, while ignoring other figures that might lead to a different conclusion. The amount of available data makes all the difference; the more numbers to choose among, the more certain one is to find some potentially useful "cherries," ripe for the picking. All manner of interested parties can adopt the tactic of cherry-picking. Political incumbents can point with pride to evidence of improvements during their tenure in office, even as their challengers argue that the facts show that things have deteriorated (and will likely get even worse unless the voters oust the rascals). Similarly, proponents of particular ideologies can select figures that seem to confirm their ideas.

Without inspecting the original data, it can be hard to detect cherry-picking, although one suspicious sign is when advocates of some position offer very specific numbers in support of a broad argument. For example, someone might declare, "Between 1997 and 2000, the percentage of high school seniors who reported trying heroin during the previous thirty days rose by 40 percent!" While this is true (reported usage rose from 0.5 to 0.7 percent, a 40 percent increase), the speaker ignores data from the same MTF reports showing that the seniors' reported use of most other drugs, including marijuana, cocaine, alcohol, and cigarettes, fell. But only the most careful listener might think to ask why the speaker chose to focus on one specific drug (particularly on one rarely used by high school students).

Statistics, then, can be both the subjects of spinning, and—when carefully selected through cherry-picking—tools for spinners. Spinning may feature pretty good numbers, but because these figures appear out of context, complexity and nuance have been stripped away. The statistics then can serve to promote the viewpoint of whoever injects them into an ongoing debate. The point is not that some numbers are correct and others have been "spun"; rather, it is to caution us that every number presented in public debates may have been plucked from all the available figures because an advocate saw it as having rhetorical potential. Whenever numbers seem to offer especially powerful support to a particular position in a debate over a social issue, we need to be alert for signs of spinning or cherry-picking.

Advocates who spin statistics recognize that numbers can have symbolic significance in debates over social issues. Answering even the simplest questions—How many? A lot or only a little?—can have powerful symbolic importance because different answers can seem to lend support to one side or another in social conflicts. Consider recent disputes over the size of two religious populations—Muslims and Jews—in the United States. At first glance, the number of adherents to a particular religion might not seem like a topic that would generate intense interest; the number of Presbyterians, for instance, does not command much attention outside that denomination. But because the numbers of Jews and Muslims in this country may have implications for how Americans think about the Israeli-Palestinian conflict, terrorism, and other foreign policy concerns, as well as about the future prospects for these religions in the United States, various groups have been bickering about both these estimates.

The number of Muslims in the United States became a hot topic after the September 11, 2001, terrorist attacks. Some worried that the government or the public might blame all Muslims for the attacks, leading to a wave of anti-Muslim hate crimes or even repressive policies akin to the relocation of Japanese Americans during World War II. There also was a sense among some advocates that Muslims needed to be recognized as a substantial religious minority within the United States, so that their interests and concerns might warrant more consideration.

Recent estimates for the U.S. Muslim population range from

fewer than two million to close to ten million. This may seem like a remarkable range, but remember (as noted in chapter 1) that the census—usually the most authoritative source for population statistics—does not gather information on religion. Thus, it is necessary to find other ways to derive estimates. Some analysts have used national origin as a basis for calculations; they assume that people whose ancestors (or who themselves) came from largely Muslim countries are themselves Muslim. Others have tried to calculate the number of mosques in the United States, multiply that number by some average number of people affiliated with each mosque, and then add an estimate for Muslims unaffiliated with any mosque. Still other analysts derive their data from surveys that ask respondents to state their religion. Each of these methods has limitations. For example, religious affiliation among immigrants may not reflect the overall pattern of religious affiliation among the population in their country of origin (just as immigrants to colonial Massachusetts were far more likely to be Puritans than the general English population). It is also difficult to identify all mosques, to judge estimates of the average number affiliated with a mosque, and to assess the estimates of unaffiliated Muslims. And, of course, because not everyone cooperates with surveys, survey results may undercount the populations they seek to measure.[14]

The methods favored—and the critiques of rival methods—differ depending on one's position in the larger debate. Several major Muslim organizations, for example, with an understandable interest in showing that their religion has many adherents, sponsored a study based on mosques. The study concluded that about two million people were associated with mosques and then, assuming that an even larger number of Muslims were not

involved in mosques, argued that the overall Muslim population was between six and seven million. Some Jewish organizations countered that this estimate was unreasonably high and
pointed to survey results suggesting a total figure just below two
million. Muslims, in turn, suggested that surveys undercount
respondents who, for reasons of fear or language barriers, fail to
report their religion to interviewers. One cannot help but suspect that the number of Jews (estimated at between five and
six million) serves as an important benchmark in this debate:
Muslim organizations favor estimates that place the number of
Muslims as greater than the number of Jews, whereas Jewish
organizations prefer figures that suggest that Jews outnumber
Muslims.

Although recent efforts to estimate the size of the Muslim
population attracted widespread interest, debate over the number of Jews in the United States, while intense, has remained
largely confined to the Jewish community. Here, the concern is
not only that Jews are a small religious minority but also that
their numbers may actually be declining, which has led some
commentators to warn that American Jews may be "vanishing."[15] This concern, which has a long history, intensified after
reports of recent social research. In both 1990 and 2000, major
Jewish organizations sponsored the National Jewish Population
Surveys (NJPS), large-scale research efforts designed to measure the Jewish population. These surveys revealed that a slight
majority of Jews were marrying non-Jews (raising the prospect
that children from these marriages might not be raised as Jews)
and that Jewish women bore an average of 1.8 children (that is,
below the level needed to replace the Jewish population).
Especially controversial was the news that the 2000 estimate for

the Jewish population (5.2 million) was actually lower than the 1990 figure (5.5 million). Critics charged that the NJPS had badly undercounted the Jewish population, that the correct total was closer to 6.7 million.

This debate hinged on disagreements about how best to define who is Jewish. Is it a matter of religious practice? Or are Jews those who think of themselves as Jewish? The NJPS counted both categories. But what about people who say they were once but are no longer Jewish, or who live in households with others who report being Jewish? People in these categories, excluded by the NJPS, were counted in the critics' estimates. In addition, the critics argued that fear of anti-Semitism would have led some NJPS respondents to deny being Jewish. As always, a narrow definition will produce a smaller estimate than a broad definition.

At one level, debates over estimates of the numbers of Muslims and Jews in the United States can be seen as questions of method and definition. If we try to count Muslims by estimating how many people are affiliated with mosques and then add an estimate for the unaffiliated, we get one (high) number; if we use survey research, we get a second (lower) figure. Similarly, defining Jewish identity narrowly produces a lower estimate than adopting a broader definition. On a technical level, social scientists can debate the advantages and limitations of the different methods and definitions. (The consensus would probably favor using surveys to estimate the Muslim population and the narrower NJPS definition to identify Jews, but not everyone would agree.) But, of course, these are not merely technical questions. These statistics have symbolic importance—to argue that a group is large or growing may suggest that its interests should be more important than those of a group that is smaller or shrinking. And commitment to such political messages can lead to impassioned defenses of numbers that might not receive strong support on purely technical grounds.

THE RESULTS OF WELFARE REFORM

The 1996 federal welfare reform law (the Personal Responsibility and Work Opportunity Reconciliation Act, or PRWORA) was the product of decades of bitter debate. Most often, critics of welfare complained that the system fostered long-term dependency, that some recipients not only remained on welfare but also raised children who, in turn, would themselves spend their adult lives on welfare, in a troubling intergenerational cycle. The central argument was that welfare discouraged self-reliance and personal responsibility and that it had become self-perpetuating. In contrast, defenders of welfare insisted that it was necessary, that it was a vital safety net providing minimal protection for individuals who had too few resources to provide for themselves in a society that otherwise offered limited opportunities. Rather than seeing welfare recipients as individuals who failed to exercise responsibility, they blamed a social system that featured too few jobs and too much discrimination.

Both welfare's critics and its defenders understood that welfare was linked to other social problems: recipients were, by definition, poor; in addition, they tended to have less education and more serious health problems than those not receiving welfare. Many women on welfare bore their children out of wedlock, and the fathers of their children often lacked jobs. To the critics, welfare discouraged work and marriage; to the defenders, the absence of decent employment opportunities created the social circumstances that forced people to turn to and stay on welfare. Defenders called for more benefits to improve recipients' standard of living, as well as job training and other programs to improve their prospects, while critics charged that raising benefits and expanding programs only fostered dependency. The debate stretched over decades.

PRWORA—the product of a Republican-controlled Congress and signed by President Bill Clinton—was designed to "end welfare as we know it." In particular, the new law replaced the old Aid to Families with Dependent Children (AFDC) entitlement with Temporary Assistance for Needy Families (TANF) block grants to the states, giving the states considerable discretion in designing arrangements to help the poor. In addition, the new law established a lifetime limit for most recipients of no more than sixty months of cash assistance from federal funds, and it required that recipients work after receiving two years of cash assistance.

These were billed as significant, dramatic changes. The new law's supporters (mostly conservatives) envisioned a rosy future in which the formerly dependent would learn personal responsibility, take charge of their lives, and work their way up from poverty. Its critics (mostly liberals) warned of an impending social catastrophe in which declining support would force millions of people into poverty and increase the ranks of the homeless. Supporters promoted the new law as providing encouragement; critics insisted that it would be harsh and punitive.

The fifth anniversary of the welfare reform legislation—a significant date because it marked the passing of sixty months (PRWORA's lifetime limit for cash assistance)—provided an occasion to assess the law's impact.[16] Supporters presented numerous statistics as evidence that welfare reform had been a success: the number of households receiving assistance was down from AFDC's 1994 peak of 5.1 million to about 2 million; the proportion of single mothers who were working had risen; and the proportion of births to unmarried mothers—which had risen rapidly during the years just preceding welfare reform—had barely increased. Even PRWORA's most vigorous critics had to concede that, at least so far, the predicted catastrophe had not occurred.

What had happened? Analysts concluded that the overall statistics were affected by several developments. The first was good timing: the early years of welfare reform occurred during an economic boom, when unemployment was low and jobs were relatively plentiful. Second, and probably more important, although this effort was less publicized than welfare reform, the federal government had instituted or expanded policies that were designed to assist low-income workers, such as the Earned Income Tax Credit (EITC), increased aid for child care, and expanded access to Medicaid. Since much of the public hostility to welfare centered on the recipients' failure to work, these programs to assist people who were working had much broader support. The increased benefits provided by these programs meant that at least some low-income workers who in the past might have been forced to go on welfare to qualify for needed support (say, to deal with a child's medical bills) now could remain employed.

Much was made of the number of recipients who left the welfare rolls, but this was in some ways a selective reading of the evidence. It had always been the case that most recipients received only short-term aid; people had been going off welfare during every year of the program's history. It was difficult to establish whether there had been a marked increase in the numbers of people who left the welfare rolls—post-PRWORA record-keepers carefully counted their numbers, but the records of earlier years were less complete. The real difference may have been a third factor: PRWORA, which allowed states to set standards for eligibility, made it harder to qualify for welfare benefits. Instead of being added to the welfare rolls in the first place, would-be recipients might be urged to apply for jobs or required to fulfill other requirements that had the effect of encouraging them to consider options other than going on welfare.

Different commentators weighed these factors differently, in fairly predictable ways. Welfare reform's critics tended to emphasize the importance of the healthy economy for the program's apparent success (and they watched with foreboding as the economic boom ended). They also noted the importance of the various programs to support the working poor (which were generally more popular with liberals than with conservatives). In contrast, PRWORA's supporters argued that the program's success revealed that welfare had been unnecessary in many cases, and they called for new reforms to restrict benefits further.

Still other critics suggested that the overall assessment of success overlooked evidence indicating that welfare reform had had harmful consequences for some of the poor. In 2003, for example, the Children's Defense Fund (CDF) noted that, although the proportion of black children living in families officially defined as poor had dropped markedly since 1995, the number of black children being raised in "extreme poverty" (which the CDF defined as households with incomes no more than half the federal poverty line) increased sharply between 2000 and 2001.[17] The report generated sympathetic editorials about the plight of "the poorest of the poor" in some newspapers as well as accusations of cherry-picking. (One conservative charged that the CDF had "searched with a laser for something negative to say, because the poverty picture in America since the 1996 welfare reform is unambiguously positive.") But, of course, we needn't presume that a policy change such as welfare reform will have the same effect on every person. Complicated problems are not likely to have simple solutions, any more than they are likely to have simple causes.

Social policies such as PRWORA are relatively blunt instruments designed to address problems that usually involve complicated tangles of causes and consequences. When people have disagreed over whether introducing a policy would be desirable or ill advised, they are unlikely to agree about its effects. Again, the notion of trade-offs is relevant: every policy is likely to have benefits and costs, and its proponents can be expected to praise the benefits, even as their opponents decry the costs. This complexity should make us wary of simplistic policy assessments that pronounce success or failure, as evidenced by one or two statistics. Complexity cannot be summarized in a couple of magical, cherry-picked numbers, and we should question claims that make everything seem simple and straightforward.

QUARRELING OVER NUMBERS

Americans have a widespread, naive faith in the power of numbers to resolve debates, to provide facts that can overpower opposition. This faith rests on some dubious assumptions. The first is a belief that numbers are by nature factual, that they constitute incontrovertible evidence. This ignores an even more basic truth—that all numbers are products of human efforts. We cannot escape the fact that statistics are social constructions.

Recognizing this means that we can't treat numbers as straightforward bits of truth; rather, we must be critical, asking who counted what, and how, and why. But it does not mean that we can't trust any statistics, that we should treat them all as equally worthless. There are better and worse ways of counting, and we can have more confidence in some numbers than in others. All science is not junk science; with a little effort—and the patience to wait for more information—we can distinguish between the two.

A second weak assumption is that our side's numbers are better than the other side's numbers, simply because they're ours. Our positions, biases, political ideologies, and perspectives shape how we approach evidence, including statistics. We have a natural tendency to welcome numbers that reaffirm what we believe to be true. Precisely because these figures are consistent with our view of the world, we tend to downplay—if not be oblivious to—their weaknesses. We give them a sympathetic reading, a free ride. In contrast, our critical faculties swing into operation when we confront numbers that challenge our beliefs. Now we ask the hard questions: What could have led to numbers that are so obviously wrong? Was it peculiar definitions? Faulty methods? Bad samples? Inappropriate analysis? There is nothing like a discomforting statistic to help most of us uncover critical abilities we might not have realized we had.

This chapter also suggests a third consideration: social life is complicated. While discussions of some social problems are one-sided (child molestation and serial murder have few defenders), other issues lead to debates among people with different assumptions, beliefs, attitudes, and values. Debaters commonly unveil statistics that support their positions, and of course they find their own numbers convincing, even as they express deep reservations about their opponents' figures. Whether we are actively engaged in these debates or somewhere on the sidelines, it may help to consider the possibility of complexity. The choices that people make in counting are necessary and are undoubtedly shaped by many factors—some methods of counting are cheaper than others, some are a better fit for the people doing the counting, some may seem more likely to lead to the results they hope to find. We should expect that the choices people make shape their results.

We shouldn't presume that most social issues are simple to understand. If they were all that simple, we wouldn't have all that disagreement. When we encounter disagreements about the validity of a number, or when we hear people promoting rival numbers, we ought to consider the possibility that there may be an underlying complexity—that instead of trying to decide which side owns the truth, we might be better off trying to reconcile the competing claims, to understand how and why people have different visions of what's true. We may, of course, decide in favor of one position, but then we may also come to understand that it's a little more complicated than that.

Bad statistics aren't rare. You can probably spot at least one dubious number in this morning's newspaper. Recognizing bad statistics is not all that difficult; it takes clear thinking more than it requires any advanced mathematical knowledge. And most people will agree that we ought to stamp out bad statistics.

Still, bad numbers flourish. Why? Shouldn't we be able to teach "statistical literacy"—basic skills for critically interpreting the sorts of statistics we encounter in everyday life? Why can't statistical literacy be part of the standard high school or college curriculum? Shouldn't we be able to, in effect, immunize young people so that they will be able to think critically about the numbers they encounter and resist bad statistics?

Every year, thousands of high school seniors enroll in Advanced Placement statistics classes. (At the end of the year, these students can take the national AP statistics exam, and, if they score well enough, many colleges will give them credit for having completed a basic statistics course.) Many thousands more students will take at least one statistics course in college. We might expect that statistical literacy would be an important part of these courses.

We would be wrong. Statistics textbooks, as well as the AP exam, all but ignore the sorts of issues raised in this book. Rather, statistics instruction, in both high school and college, focuses on what I call matters of *calculation*—on the theory and logic behind particular statistical measures, on the methods of actually computing those measures, and on the interpretation of the results. Introductory statistics textbooks feature chapters on probability theory, on tests of significance, correlation, regression, and so on. That is, these textbooks assume that the students who read them might want to use statistics to interpret data derived from some sort of scientific research. There is nothing wrong with this; those students who do become researchers will indeed need to know how to calculate those statistics.

However, such textbooks and courses say next to nothing about how to interpret the simple statistics—the graphs and numbers—the students might encounter in the morning newspaper. Why? If everyone agrees that statistical literacy is an important skill, why isn't it an important part of statistics instruction?

Statistics is usually understood as a branch of mathematics, hence the focus on calculation. I am sure that most high schools consider the AP statistics class to be a math class and assign a math teacher to teach it. The goal of the course is to make students proficient statistical calculators; the classes are not designed to make them statistically literate. To no one's surprise, math teachers believe that their job is to teach math, to teach students how to calculate correctly so that the students can score well on tests of calculation, such as the AP statistics exam.

Similarly, the statistics courses taught in college—even the basic, introductory courses—devote almost all their attention to matters of calculation. The spread of computers and easily mastered statistical software packages has encouraged the use of highly sophisticated statistics. Before 1970 or so, a person without advanced training in statistics who picked up an issue of a leading social science journal, such as the *American Sociological Review,* could probably understand the data presented in many of the articles. This is no longer true. Today's *ASR* articles feature ordinary least-squares regression, log-linear regression, and other complex, multivariate statistical techniques that probably cannot be understood by anyone who has not taken at least two semesters of statistics in college. Naturally, college instructors believe that their job is to teach students to master these advanced techniques.

Could it be that the kinds of issues I've raised in this book strike most statistics instructors (and textbook authors) as too simple to warrant comment? Perhaps. But more than that, the topics we've covered aren't matters of calculation. We have been less concerned with mathematical processes (calculations) than with a social process. Our focus has been on who counts—who produces numbers, why they produce them, which audiences consume them, and how those numbers are understood and put to use. That is, we have tried to understand the social construction of numbers more than their calculation.

But statistics classes largely ignore the ways statistics are used as evidence for understanding social issues as well as the ways people count. If the social process by which statistics are brought into being is mentioned, it is probably in relation to the idea of bias—instructors may warn students that "biased" people can devise distorted statistics. But beyond blaming bias—which is treated as a sort of contamination originating outside the mathematically pure realm of calculation—statistics classes rarely explore what this distortion might involve.

In short, even if everyone agrees that it would be desirable for students to improve their ability to think critically about the sorts of statistics found in news coverage, statistics teachers aren't likely to feel that this is their job.

ASSIGNING RESPONSIBILITY
FOR STATISTICAL LITERACY

Contemporary educators are beset by competing demands. On the one hand, as new social issues come to public attention, there are often calls to add material to the schools' curriculum; sex education and drug education are obvious examples, among many others. A school district may win a grant for an anti-bullying program. There may be campaigns at the state or school district level to make students aware of various sorts of discrimination. The list goes on and on, and it changes with each passing year. Some of these new special topics become enduring elements in the schools' curriculum, but others turn out to be short-lived enthusiasms, educational fads.

On the other hand, many grumble that schools are neglecting the basics, the Three Rs. The school accountability movement, at least in part, demands that schools return to emphasizing instruction in basic skills. Schools and teachers, then, find themselves trapped between calls to spend more time teaching basic skills and pressure to add instruction about whatever new special topics currently occupy the public's attention. The school day contains only a limited number of minutes, and all sorts of people want more minutes to be devoted to whatever topics they deem important.

So a first question might be whether statistical literacy ought to be considered an additional special topic or a basic skill. If it is promoted as a special topic—like AIDS education and bullying prevention—its long-term prospects won't be bright. This year's addition to the curriculum easily becomes a candidate for elimination when next year arrives with its calls to teach still other new topics.

Well, what if we call statistical literacy a basic skill? Certainly a plausible argument exists for considering it in these terms. After all, we are talking about teaching people to be more critical, to be more thoughtful about what they read in the newspaper or watch in a news broadcast, to ask questions about claims from scientists, politicians, or activists. Being better able to assess such claims is certainly valuable; we might even argue that it is fundamental to being an informed citizen. Why not consider statistical literacy a basic skill?

But this raises another question: what sort of basic skill is it? The answer matters because both high schools and colleges parcel out responsibility for instruction to departments organized to teach topics. A typical high school has separate departments for science, social sciences, mathematics, English, and so on; most colleges subdivide many of these broad categories, for example, assigning the responsibility for teaching to separate departments for biology, chemistry, and so on. In general, the larger the educational institution, the more departments it recognizes.

Departments are natural competitors. While everyone may acknowledge the value of a well-rounded education, each department tends to assume that it plays an especially important role. And because money is always short, departments compete for available funds to hire faculty and purchase equipment. It is the rare department that doesn't want to expand; in particular, many departments would like to offer more advanced training, such as AP courses in high schools or graduate programs in colleges.

This competition means that teaching basic skills often is devalued. For example, almost all of the thousands of first-year students admitted to large universities each year are required to take an English composition class. Those classes need to be small, because the students must write a lot of papers, and those papers need to be graded quickly and carefully. At most universities, the job of teaching those composition classes falls on graduate students or part-time instructors, not on English professors. In part, it is much cheaper to teach composition this way; in part, English professors prefer to teach advanced courses to English majors (because both the subject matter and the students are more interesting). The point is that teaching this basic skill is not considered particularly rewarding. (Some universities' English departments have spun off separate departments of composition, writing centers, or other programs to handle this unpleasant chore.)

The example of English composition can help us appreciate the problems of teaching statistical literacy. College instructors are well aware that substantial proportions of students have trouble reading—let alone thinking critically about—basic graphs or tables. This is a very important skill because graphs and tables are certain to appear in much of the reading a student will need to do in the course of college. And yet, no one wants to teach this skill, or at least to spend much time doing so. Many have the sense that students should already be proficient in these skills when they get to college (even though it is clear that many are not). To many others, it seems too simple, too basic—a waste of time for professors who would prefer to teach the more advanced topics in their disciplines.

In addition, the spread of personal computers and sophisticated software helps sustain the illusion that students already understand this stuff. Anyone who visits a junior high school science fair will see all manner of eye-catching, computer-generated graphs. As long as no one bothers to ask whether these graphs are clear and useful (they often are neither), it is easy to be impressed by what the students have produced. Similarly, students learn that they can find answers to pretty much any question by searching the Internet. They may not locate particularly good answers, but they find answers all the same. The experience that many students already have in using high-tech methods (albeit to produce low-quality results) helps to justify claims that we don't need to teach basic skills, that we can move on to teaching more interesting, advanced material.

Thus, statistics and mathematics instructors are unlikely to have any more interest in teaching statistical literacy than English professors have in teaching first-year composition. Nor are other departments eager to teach this material. I teach sociology courses, but I know that most sociology professors tend to dismiss statistical literacy as "not really sociology"; faculty in psychology and other disciplines probably have the same reaction. Statistical literacy falls between the stools on which academic departments perch.

There is precedent to support my pessimism. During the late 1980s and early 1990s, "critical thinking" became a buzzword on college campuses. This should have been the perfect slogan around which to rally support for educational reform. Virtually all professors consider themselves critical thinkers, and most would agree that students must learn to think more critically— another highly desirable basic skill. But because all those professors believed that they already were teaching their students to think critically (even though they simultaneously complained that many students were poor critical thinkers), and because no department wanted to take on the responsibility for teaching the topic across the campus, interest in improving critical thinking peaked, and the strength of the idea as an educational slogan has begun to fade.

What happened to critical thinking? Why didn't that good idea become an enduring part of education in all schools? The lack of a departmental "owner," a department that would house, protect, and nurture critical thinking, meant that teaching the skill remained everyone's responsibility—and therefore no one's.

This example suggests that a specific department needs to take responsibility for teaching statistical literacy. As we have already established, this is not likely to be a mathematics or statistics program, however logical that might seem at first glance. The social sciences might offer an alternative home. After all, issues of statistical literacy often emerge around discussions of social issues. But again, sociology professors are likely to dismiss statistical literacy as not being "real sociology" (and other departments may react the same way).

Departmental organization offers considerable advantages for educational institutions, but it also carries costs. It is difficult to teach subjects that do not fit neatly within what a department considers its proper instructional domain. This helps to explain why many graduates of high schools and colleges remain uncomfortable when confronted with even basic statistics—and why this situation will not change easily. The lessons involved in teaching statistical literacy are not so terribly difficult; rather, the difficulty lies in finding someone willing to teach them.

THE STATISTICAL LITERACY MOVEMENT

Despite these obstacles, a small educational movement advocating statistical literacy has emerged. Professor Milo Schield, director of the W. M. Kleck Foundation Statistical Literacy Project at Augsburg College in Minneapolis, is the movement's leading voice. Schield operates the Statistical Literacy Web site (www.StatLit.org); for those interested in statistical literacy as an educational movement, the site includes a section on teaching. Although this is a promising development, the campaign to promote formal instruction in statistical literacy is in its early phases.

But perhaps statistical literacy doesn't have to be taught in classrooms. Recently, there seem to be increasing calls to promote statistical literacy outside the educational establishment. Consider, for example, these resources:

· The Statistical Assessment Service (www.stats.org) has been criticizing the media's handling of statistics since 1995. SAS published newsletters until 2002, when it converted to distributing its reports on its Web site. A book based on SAS analyses is both readable and available in paperback; see David Murray, Joel Schwartz, and S. Robert Lichter, *It Ain't Necessarily So: How Media Make and Unmake the Scientific Picture of Reality* (2001).

· Various Web sites from around the world feature discussions of bad statistics. Some of these contain mostly original material; others are little more than links to specific discussions around the Web. Numberwatch (www.numberwatch.co.uk) is a British site; its operator, John Brignell, is the author of *Sorry, Wrong Number! The Abuse of Measurement* (2000). The Social Issues Research Centre (www.sirc.org) is another British site presenting analyses of issues that often involve critiques of statistics. Pénombre (www.penombre.org) is a French site, which also contains some materials in English. The Canadian Statistical Assessment Service (www.canstats.org) resembles its U.S. counterpart, while another Canadian site, Innumeracy.com (www.innumeracy.com), is basically a catalog of links. Numeracy in the News, an Australian site, is aimed at educators and students; it features sample articles, graphs, and so on, each accompanied by study questions and commentary (http://ink.news.com.au/mercury/ mathguys/mercury .htm). Many of these organizations also offer links to more specialized sites, including official statistics (many government agencies now provide sites where one can access their statistical reports) and sites devoted to particular social issues or types of data—for example, Quackwatch (www.quackwatch.org) on medical claims, Junkscience.com (www.junkscience.com) on media coverage of scientific news, and the Center for Media and Democracy (www.prwatch.org) for critiques of industry and government public relations campaigns. As might be expected, such sites vary in their concerns and underlying ideologies, and their critiques should be examined critically rather than simply being accepted.

· It's often fun to explore bad statistics, but for sheer entertainment, it is hard to beat Cecil Adams's column, "The Straight Dope," which appears in alternative weekly newspapers. Its motto is "Fighting Ignorance Since 1973 (It's Taking Longer Than We Thought)." Each week, Adams addresses one or more questions—often on topics that good taste leads other media to ignore; some, although by no means all, involve sorting out statistical claims. The Web site (www.straightdope.com) offers an index for and access to all the columns. If you're interested in exotic topics, this is a wonderful resource.

· Other media commentators also promote statistical literacy. The mathematician John Allen Paulos, author of *Innumeracy: Mathematical Illiteracy and Its Consequences* (2001) and other books for general readers, has a Web site (http://euclid.math .temple.edu/~paulos/) that links to his various works, including his columns for ABC.com. The British Broadcasting Corporation has several mathematically themed radio programs, including "More or Less," which features frequent commentaries on statistical issues. Broadcasts are archived at http://news.bbc.co .uk/1/hi/programmes/more_or_less/archive/default.stm.

· The American Statistical Association publishes *Chance,* a quarterly magazine devoted to interesting uses of statistics. Some of the articles require considerable background in statistics, but others are more accessible. As an introduction to what professional statisticians do, it is a valuable resource.

· Many books on statistical topics are available, ranging from textbooks that teach students how to calculate different statistics to volumes—such as this one—that offer critiques of how statistics are used and misused in contemporary society. (Several of these books are listed in the notes to earlier chapters of this volume.)

These various sources form a chorus of voices promoting the cause of statistical literacy. Of course, disagreements arise within the movement. Some advocates have ideological agendas: conservatives concentrate on exposing liberals' misuse of statistics, while liberals attack dubious numbers promoted by conservatives. Some critics seem to blame "the media" for irresponsibly publicizing bad statistics, but journalists—not unreasonably—respond that they often have no good way to assess the numbers their sources offer. Some statisticians advocate better mathematical training to improve our understanding of calculation, while social scientists (such as myself) argue that it is important to locate numbers within the social context that creates and disseminates them.

In short, it may be true that "everyone" agrees that improving statistical literacy is desirable, but it isn't clear that they can agree on what statistical literacy means, what improving it might involve, or what the consequences of this improvement might be.

Even if no one opposes statistical literacy, serious obstacles remain. There is disagreement about which skills need to be taught, and, at least so far, no group has offered to take responsibility for doing the necessary teaching. Plenty of information is out there—any interested individual can learn ways to think more critically about statistics—but the statistical literacy movement has yet to convince most educators that they need to change what the educational system is doing.

Many of us kid ourselves that bad statistics come from people with whom we disagree, and we fantasize that improving statistical literacy will inevitably swell the ranks of people who agree with us, that all critical thinkers will recognize the flaws in our opponents' arguments, while finding our claims convincing.

I wouldn't count on things working out that way. Statistical literacy is a tool, and, like most tools, it can be used for many purposes. If more people think more critically about statistics, they are likely to use that skill to criticize our numbers as well as those of our opponents. When everyone's numbers come under scrutiny, we are all held to higher standards.

But that's not bad. As things stand, we constantly find ourselves exposed to lots of statistics. Some of those numbers are pretty good, but many aren't. As a result, we worry about things that probably aren't worth the trouble, even as we ignore things that ought to warrant our attention. Improving statistical literacy—if we can manage it—could help us tell the difference and, in a small way, make us wiser.

PREFACE

1. Some readers may recall that I made a similar statement in *Damned Lies and Statistics: Untangling Numbers from the Media, Politicians, and Activists* (Berkeley: University of California Press, 2001), p. 27. This book presents different examples, organized in a different way, and I have tried to minimize the overlap, but the underlying approach is the same. You needn't have read the first book to understand this one, however; the two are intended to complement each other.

2. Darrell Huff, *How to Lie with Statistics* (New York: Norton, 1954); Gerald E. Jones, *How to Lie with Charts* (San Francisco: Sybex, 1995); Mark Monmonier, *How to Lie with Maps* (Chicago: University of Chicago Press, 1991); Robert Hooke, *How to Tell the Liars from the Statisticians* (New York: Marcel Dekker, 1983); Richard P. Runyon, *How Numbers Lie* (Lexington, Mass.: Lewis, 1981); Best, *Damned Lies and Statistics;* also: Tukufu Zuberi, *Thicker than Blood: How Racial Statistics Lie* (Minneapolis: University of Minnesota Press, 2001). Other books have chapters on the theme: see, for example, "Statistics and Damned Lies," in A. K. Dewdney, *200% of Nothing* (New York: Wiley, 1993),

pp. 23–42. In addition, a recent three-hundred-page book designed to help statistics instructors reach their students includes a seventeen-page chapter entitled "Lying with Statistics," which addresses issues of bias; see Andrew Gelman and Deborah Nolan, *Teaching Statistics: A Bag of Tricks* (New York: Oxford University Press, 2002), pp. 147–163.

CHAPTER 1. MISSING NUMBERS

1. Rather is quoted in Lynnell Hancock, "The School Shootings: Why Context Counts," *Columbia Journalism Review* 40 (May 2001): 76. Much has been published about these episodes, and particularly on the Columbine shootings. See, for example, Daniel M. Filler, "Random Violence and the Transformation of the Juvenile Justice Debate," *Virginia Law Review* 86 (2000): 1095–1125; and Gary Kleck, "There Are No Lessons to Be Learned from Littleton," *Criminal Justice Ethics* 18 (Winter 1999): 2, 61–63.

2. Relevant compilations of evidence regarding school violence include Margaret Small and Kellie Dressler Tetrick, "School Violence: An Overview," *Juvenile Justice* (U.S. Office of Juvenile Justice and Delinquency Prevention) 8 (June 2001): 3–12; Phillip Kaufman et al., *Indicators of School Crime and Safety: 2001* (Washington, D.C.: U.S. Departments of Education and Justice, 2001); Kim Brooks, Vincent Schiraldi, and Jason Ziedenberg, *School House Hype: Two Years Later* (Washington, D.C.: Justice Policy Institute, 1999); National School Safety Center, *School Associated Violent Deaths,* 2001, available at www .nssc1.org; and Mark Anderson et al., "School-Associated Violent Deaths in the United States, 1994–1999," *Journal of the American Medical Association* 286 (December 5, 2001): 2695–2702. For information about journalists' standards for assessing crime statistics, see Kurt Silver, *Understanding Crime Statistics: A Reporter's Guide* (n.p.: Investigative Reporters and Editors Inc., 2000).

3. Chip Heath, Chris Bell, and Emily Sternberg, "Emotional Selection in Memes: The Case of Urban Legends," *Journal of Personality and Social Psychology* 81 (2001): 1028–1041.

4. Cynthia J. Bogard, *Seasons Such as These* (Hawthorne, N.Y.: Aldine de Gruyter, 2003).

5. Compare Kiron K. Skinner, Annelise Anderson, and Martin Anderson, *Reagan, in His Own Hand* (New York: Free Press, 2001), pp. 241, 459; and Tip O'Neill, *Man of the House* (New York: Random House, 1987), pp. 347–348.

6. In response, welfare critics offered their own numbers suggesting that abuses were widespread. One analysis suggested: "A major source of the variations among estimates [for welfare fraud] . . . has been the estimators' use of very different definitions of improprieties" (John A. Gardiner and Theodore R. Lyman, *The Fraud Control Game* [Bloomington: Indiana University Press, 1984], p. 2).

7. On the 1980s, see Joel Best, *Threatened Children* (Chicago: University of Chicago Press, 1990). On 2002, see Donna Leinwand, "Kidnapping Problem 'Impossible' to Quantify," *USA Today,* August 15, 2002, p. 3A.

8. For an introduction to this approach, see Anthony E. Boardman et al., *Cost-Benefit Analysis: Concepts and Practice* (Upper Saddle River, N.J.: Prentice Hall, 1996).

9. For a critique of one oft-repeated tale of amoral cost-benefit analysts, see Matthew T. Lee and M. David Ermann, "Pinto 'Madness' as a Flawed Landmark Narrative," *Social Problems* 46 (1999): 30–47.

10. Viviana A. Zelizer, *Pricing the Priceless Child* (New York: Basic Books, 1985).

11. William Petersen, *Ethnicity Counts* (New Brunswick, N.J.: Transaction, 1997), pp. 78–81.

12. C. Kirk Hadaway, Penny Long Marler, and Mark Chaves, "What the Polls Don't Show: A Closer Look at U.S. Church Attendance," *American Sociological Review* 58 (1993): 741–752.

13. On the 2000 census, see Margo Anderson and Stephen E. Fienberg, "Census 2000 and the Politics of Census Taking," *Society* 39 (November 2001): 17–25; and Eric Schmitt, "For 7 Million People in Census, One Race Category Isn't Enough," *New York Times,* March 13, 2001, p. A1. For historical background, see Petersen, *Ethnicity Counts.*

14. For the basic arguments about how to measure unemployment, see David Leonhardt, "Breadline? What Breadline?" *New York Times,* June 24, 2001, sec. 4, p. 5; and Leonhardt, "Help Wanted: Out of a Job and No Longer Looking," *New York Times,* September 29, 2002, sec. 4, p. 1.

15. Fox Butterfield, "When Police Shoot, Who's Counting?" *New York Times,* April 29, 2001, sec. 4, p. 5. For a more general critique of how politics can shape what officials choose not to count, see A. P. Tant, "The Politics of Official Statistics," *Government and Opposition* 30 (1995): 254–266.

16. For a case study of how political considerations can shape the ways an official agency (the Canadian Centre for Justice Statistics) collects, analyzes, and presents data, see Kevin D. Haggerty, *Making Crime Count* (Toronto: University of Toronto Press, 2001).

17. American Medical Association, Office of Alcohol and Other Drug Abuse, "College Binge-Drinking Prevention Program Calls on *Princeton Review* to Stop Publishing 'Party Schools List,'" press release, August 7, 2002.

18. Bureau of the Census, *Historical Statistics of the United States* (Washington, D.C., 1975), p. 58.

19. On some of the ways progress serves to make us more conscious of social problems, see Joel Best, "Social Progress and Social Problems," *Sociological Quarterly* 42 (2001): 1–12.

20. The spread of the falling-coconuts statistic was aided by a British travel insurer; see Beverly Beckham, "Travelers Should Watch Out for Coconuts: The Killer Fruit," *Boston Herald,* April 7, 2002, p. 30. A discussion of the available data appeared on Cecil Adams's splendid Web site "The Straight Dope" on July 19, 2002; see www.straightdope.com/clumns/020719.

21. Lawrence K. Altman, "Stop Those Presses! Blonds, It Seems, Will Survive After All," *New York Times,* October 2, 2002, p. A5.

22. Robert Schoen and Robin M. Weinick, "The Slowing Metabolism of Marriage: Figures from 1988 U.S. Marital Status Life Tables," *Demography* 30 (1993): 737–746. The earliest statement of this erro-

neous statistic I have found appears in Judy Klemesrud, "'If Your Face Isn't Young': Women Confront Problems of Aging," *New York Times,* October 10, 1980, p. A24.

23. Edward M. Eveld, "Awash in Water: Eight Glasses a Day? It's Probably More Than We Need, Scientists Say," *Seattle Times,* July 13, 2003, p. L6.

24. For a thorough discussion of this example, see Jonathan Marks, *What It Means to Be 98% Chimpanzee: Apes, People, and Their Genes* (Berkeley: University of California Press, 2002).

CHAPTER 2. CONFUSING NUMBERS

1. Cal Thomas, "Democrats Are Losing Center," *Wilmington (Del.) News Journal,* August 3, 2003, p. A11.

2. For examples of claims made by proponents and opponents of the tax cut, see David E. Rosenbaum, "Washington Memo: The President's Tax Cut and Its Unspoken Numbers," *New York Times,* February 25, 2003, p. A25.

3. For an introduction to the concept, see John Allen Paulos, *Innumeracy: Mathematical Illiteracy and Its Consequences* (New York: Random House, 1988).

4. Issues of definition and measurement are discussed in Best, *Damned Lies and Statistics,* pp. 39–52.

5. After inventing this example, I discovered that studies of the relationship between sinistrality (left-handedness) and delinquency do exist. Some report evidence that the two are related (although not as powerfully as my imaginary data suggest), but there seems to be no agreement about why this might be true. See, for instance, William C. Grace, "Strength of Handedness as an Indicant of Delinquents' Behavior," *Journal of Clinical Psychology* 43 (1987): 151–155.

6. It is usually legitimate, however, to compare two or more changes, expressed as percentages, that occurred during the same period. That is, if we measure the rates for two different crimes in 1980 and again in 1990, and our data show that crime X rose 25 percent,

while crime Y rose 50 percent, we can conclude that crime Y rose faster than crime X.

7. For a review of the relevant literature, see Willie Langeland and Christina Hartgers, "Child Sexual and Physical Abuse and Alcoholism," *Journal of Studies on Alcohol* 59 (1998): 336–348.

8. For a detailed discussion of the gateway concept, see Robert J. MacCoun and Peter Reuter, *Drug War Heresies* (New York: Cambridge University Press, 2001), pp. 345–351.

9. Heather Hammer, David Finkelhor, and Andrea J. Sedlak, "Children Abducted by Family Members: National Estimates and Characteristics," *National Incidence Studies of Missing, Abducted, Runaway, and Thrownaway Children* (U.S. Office of Juvenile Justice and Delinquency Prevention, October 2002).

10. Everyone can profit from reading Edward Tufte's magnificent book *The Visual Display of Quantitative Information* (Cheshire, Conn.: Graphics Press, 1983). A large, related literature includes Jones, *How to Lie with Charts;* and Howard Wainer, *Visual Revelations* (New York: Springer-Verlag, 1997).

11. A fine introduction to the principle that the areas of two-dimensional figures must be proportional to the values represented appears in Huff, *How to Lie with Statistics,* pp. 66–73.

12. Stephanie J. Ventura, T. J. Mathews, and Brady E. Hamilton, "Births to Teenagers in the United States, 1940–2000," *National Vital Statistics Reports* 49, no. 10 (September 25, 2001): 1.

13. For an example of one such critique, see Bjorn Lomborg, *The Skeptical Environmentalist* (Cambridge: Cambridge University Press, 2001), pp. 22–23.

CHAPTER 3. SCARY NUMBERS

1. Lina Guzman, Laura Lippman, Kristin Anderson Moore, and William O'Hare, "How Children Are Doing: The Mismatch Between Public Perception and Statistical Reality," *Child Trends Research Brief* (July 2003).

2. On the history of this issue, see Harold C. Sox Jr. and Steven Woloshin, "How Many Deaths Are Due to Medical Error? Getting the Number Right," *Effective Clinical Practice* 3 (2000): 277–282.

3. Warren Wolfe, "Reporting Hospital Errors Seen as Good Idea," *Minneapolis Star Tribune,* December 1, 1999, p. 3B. After citing the estimates of forty-four thousand to ninety-eight thousand annual deaths, this article notes that "medical accidents caused or contributed to 26 deaths in Minnesota hospitals between 1994 and 1997" but does not address the gulf between the very large national estimates and that state's vastly smaller number of deaths attributed to errors.

4. Rodney A. Hayward and Timothy P. Hofer, "Estimating Hospital Deaths Due to Medical Errors," *Journal of the American Medical Association* 286 (July 25, 2001): 418. This study was based on patients at veterans' hospitals, who may be older than—or otherwise differ from—patients in other hospitals.

5. For a more detailed discussion of these problems with measuring trends, see Best, *Damned Lies and Statistics,* pp. 98–109.

6. Alfred Blumstein and Joel Wallman, eds., *The Crime Drop in America* (New York: Cambridge University Press, 2000); Andrew Karmen, *New York Murder Mystery: The True Story Behind the Crime Crash of the 1990s* (New York: New York University Press, 2000).

7. For a critique of the media's coverage of this story, see David Murray, Joel Schwartz, and S. Robert Lichter, *It Ain't Necessarily So: How Media Make and Unmake the Scientific Picture of Reality* (Lanham, Md.: Rowman & Littlefield, 2001), pp. 49–52.

8. This example comes from Gerd Gigerenzer, *Calculated Risks* (New York: Simon & Schuster, 2002), p. 41.

9. A clear discussion of this point appears in John Brignell, *Sorry, Wrong Number! The Abuse of Measurement* (Great Britain: Brignell Associates, 2000), pp. 46–51. On the politics of the issue, see Gary Taubes, "Epidemiology Faces Its Limits," *Science* 269 (July 14, 1995): 164–169.

10. Cass R. Sunstein, "Probability Neglect: Emotions, Worst Cases, and Law," *Yale Law Journal* 112 (2002): 61–107.

11. Rose M. Kreider and Jason M. Fields, "Number, Timing, and

Duration of Marriages and Divorces, 1996," Bureau of the Census, *Current Population Reports,* P70–80 (Washington, D.C., February 2002). For a study based on a different sample that reaches similar conclusions, see Matthew D. Bramlett and William D. Mosher, "First Marriage Dissolution, Divorce, and Remarriage: United States," *Advance Data from Vital and Health Statistics* 323 (May 31, 2001).

12. For a more detailed discussion of these issues, see Best, "Social Progress and Social Problems."

CHAPTER 4. AUTHORITATIVE NUMBERS

1. The *Wilmington News Journal* stories (all from wire service reports) were Lindsey Tanner, "Study Takes a Rare Look at Bullying's Broad Effects," April 25, 2001, p. A1; Tammy Webber, "Sexual Solicitation Reported by 20% of Kids Who Use Web," June 20, 2001, p. A6; and Lindsey Tanner, "1 in 5 Girls Abused by a Date, Study Suggests," August 1, 2001, p. A5. The corresponding journal articles were Tonja R. Nansel et al., "Bullying Behaviors Among U.S. Youth," *Journal of the American Medical Association* 285 (April 25, 2001): 2094–2100; Kimberly J. Mitchell, David Finkelhor, and Janis Wolak, "Risk Factors for and Impact of Online Sexual Solicitation of Youth," *Journal of the American Medical Association* 285 (June 20, 2001): 3011–3014; and Jay G. Silverman et al., "Dating Violence Against Adolescent Girls and Associated Substance Abuse, Unhealthy Weight Control, Sexual Risk Behavior, Pregnancy, and Suicidality," *Journal of the American Medical Association* 286 (August 1, 2001): 572–579.

2. On the efforts of major medical journals to gain media coverage of their articles, see Ellen Ruppel Shell, "The Hippocratic Wars," *New York Times Magazine,* June 28, 1998, pp. 34–38.

3. Nels Ericson, "Addressing the Problem of Juvenile Bullying," Fact Sheet 27, June 2001, U.S. Office of Juvenile Justice and Delinquency Prevention, Washington, D.C.

4. Nansel et al., "Bullying Behaviors," p. 2095.

5. Ibid., pp. 2098, 2100.

6. Despite the quality of the NCHS data, ambiguities remain. For a discussion of these issues, see William Petersen, *From Birth to Death: A Consumer's Guide to Population Studies* (New Brunswick, N.J.: Transaction, 2000).

7. U.S. Centers for Disease Control and Prevention, "Suicide Among Black Youths: United States, 1980–1995," *Morbidity and Mortality Weekly Report* 47 (March 20, 1998): 193–196.

8. Angela G. King, "Suicides Up Among Blacks," *New York Daily News,* October 22, 2000, p. 32; M. A. J. McKenna, "Black Teen Suicide Rate Skyrockets, CDC Says," *Atlanta Constitution,* March 20, 1998, p. 1A; Mary Jo Kochakian, "Experts Can't Explain Rise in Suicide Rate Among Black Teens," *Hartford Courant,* March 31, 1998, p. F4.

9. U.S. Centers for Disease Control and Prevention, "Suicide," p. 195.

10. Most of the points raised in this discussion borrow from an analysis by the maverick sociologist Mike A. Males, whose books challenge media stereotypes about youth problems. See, for example, Males, *Framing Youth: Ten Myths About the Next Generation* (Monroe, Maine: Common Courage, 1999). I have recalculated the data, using classifications that differ somewhat from those used by Males. Compare Males, "The Myth of the (Black) Teen Suicide Epidemic," posted at www.alternet.org/story.html?StoryID=11149, July 10, 2001; and additional data posted at http://home.earthlink.net/~mmales/.

11. One revealing fact: the CDC noted that black teen suicides rose most markedly in the South. Males argues that a separate analysis of California's records shows little change over time. California has had a highly professionalized death registration program for years. In contrast, the South was slower to assign this task to medical professionals; in many Southern jurisdictions, the coroner has been an elective office, often held by an undertaker. See Males, "The Myth of the (Black) Teen Suicide Epidemic."

12. *New York Times* reporter Eric Lipton wrote a lengthy series of articles documenting the changing death toll. See, for example, these *New York Times* articles by Lipton: "Toll from Attack at Trade Center

Is Down Sharply," November 21, 2001, p. A1; "In Cold Numbers: A Census of the Sept. 11 Victims," April 19, 2002, p. A14; "Death Toll Is Near 3,000, but Some Uncertainty over the Count Remains," September 11, 2002, p. G47; and "Sept. 11 Death Toll Declines as Two People Are Found Alive," November 3, 2002, p. A17. In addition to those killed at the World Trade Center, 184 died in the Pentagon attack and 40 more in the crash of the fourth plane in Pennsylvania, but it was easier to count and identify those other victims. The deaths of the 19 hijackers were also more easily confirmed.

13. Nina Bernstein, "Thousands of Orphans? An Urban Myth," *New York Times,* October 26, 2001, p. B1.

14. Dean Baker, ed., *Getting Prices Right: The Debate over the Consumer Price Index* (Armonk, N.Y.: M. E. Sharpe, 1998); Jolie Solomon, "An Economic Speedometer Gets an Overhaul," *New York Times,* December 23, 2001, sec. 3, p. 4.

15. For example, see Norimitsu Onishi, "African Numbers, Problems, and Number Problems," *New York Times,* August 18, 2002, sec. 4, p. 5.

16. On the dark figure, see Best, *Damned Lies and Statistics,* pp. 33–34.

CHAPTER 5. MAGICAL NUMBERS

1. John M. Berry, "Number Crunchers vs. Recession: Seeking Official End, Panel Wrestles with One Stubborn Stat," *Washington Post,* July 11, 2003, p. E1; and Berry, "Recession Ended in November of 2001, But Panel Still Sees Economy Slumping," *Washington Post,* July 18, 2003, p. E1.

2. James Fallows, "The Early-Decision Racket," *Atlantic Monthly* 288 (September 2001): 37–52.

3. The formula used in 2002 is explained in Robert J. Morse and Samuel M. Flanigan, "The Rankings," *U.S. News & World Report, America's Best Colleges, 2003 Edition,* September 2002, pp. 79–81.

4. The classic work on these issues remains Harold L. Wilensky,

Organizational Intelligence: Knowledge and Policy in Government and Industry (New York: Basic Books, 1967).

5. The Soviet system has been analyzed in detail; see, for example, Stefan Hedlund, *Crisis in Soviet Agriculture* (New York: St. Martin's, 1984).

6. Alex Berenson, *The Number: How the Drive for Quarterly Earnings Corrupted Wall Street and Corporate America* (New York: Random House, 2003).

7. Mark Fazlollah, Michael Matz, and Craig R. McCoy, "How to Cut City's Crime Rate: Don't Report It," *Philadelphia Inquirer,* November 1, 1998, p. A1.

8. The Enron scandal promises to generate a huge body of literature. For an early introduction, see Loren Fox, *Enron: The Rise and Fall* (Hoboken, N.J.: Wiley, 2003).

9. Bureau of the Census, *Historical Statistics of the United States* (Washington, D.C., 1975), p. 55.

10. National Center for Education Statistics, *Digest of Education Statistics, 2001,* Table 411; posted at http://nces.ed.gov/programs/digest/do1/dt411.asp.

11. Many observers have offered competing interpretations of trends in SAT scores. For two different, rather subtle discussions, see Scott Menard, "Going Down, Going Up: Explaining the Turnaround in SAT Scores," *Youth and Society* 20 (1988): 3–28; and Charles Murray and R. J. Herrnstein, "What's Really Behind the SAT-Score Decline?" *The Public Interest* 106 (1992): 32–56.

12. A huge body of literature focuses on recent testing-centered school reforms. For example, generally favorable interpretations may be found in Williamson M. Evers and Herbert J. Walberg, eds., *School Accountability* (Stanford, Calif.: Hoover Institution Press, 2002). For a more skeptical analysis, see Laura S. Hamilton, Brian M. Stecher, and Stephen P. Klein, *Making Sense of Test-Based Accountability in Education* (Santa Monica, Calif.: Rand, 2002). On evidence of cheating, see Brian A. Jacob and Steven D. Levitt, "To Catch a Cheat," *Education Next* 4 (Winter 2004): 69–75.

13. Thomas J. Kane, Douglas O. Staiger, and Jeffrey Geppert, "Randomly Accountable," *Education Next* 2 (Spring 2002): 57–61.

14. Richard J. Lundman and Robert L. Kaufman, "Driving While Black," *Criminology* 41 (2003): 195–220.

15. Studies of racial profiling are only beginning to appear. See, for example, Robin Shepard Engel, Jennifer M. Cainon, and Thomas J. Bernard, "Theory and Racial Profiling," *Justice Quarterly* 19 (2002): 249–273; Albert J. Meehan and Michael C. Ponder, "Race and Place: The Ecology of Racial Profiling African American Motorists," *Justice Quarterly* 19 (2002): 399–430; Michael R. Smith and Geoffrey P. Alpert, "Searching for Direction: Courts, Social Science, and the Adjudication of Racial Profiling Claims," *Justice Quarterly* 19 (2002): 673–703; and Samuel Walker, "Searching for the Denominator," *Justice Research and Policy* 3 (2001): 63–95.

16. Walker, "Searching for the Denominator," 63–95.

CHAPTER 6. CONTENTIOUS NUMBERS

1. On stat wars, see Best, *Damned Lies and Statistics,* pp. 128–159.

2. On some of the more dubious recent claims to scientific status, see Robert Park, *Voodoo Science: The Road from Foolishness to Fraud* (New York: Oxford University Press, 2000).

3. For studies of some scientists' efforts to cling to marginal positions, see H. M. Collins, "Surviving Closure: Post-Rejection Adaptation and Plurality in Science," *American Sociological Review* 65 (2000): 824–845; Bart Simon, *Undead Science: Science Studies and the Afterlife of Cold Fusion* (New Brunswick, N.J.: Rutgers University Press, 2002).

4. Dorothy Nelkin, *Selling Science: How the Press Covers Science and Technology* (New York: W. H. Freeman, 1987).

5. The term came into common usage via Peter W. Huber, *Galileo's Revenge: Junk Science in the Courtroom* (New York: Basic Books, 1991).

6. Marcia Angell, *Science on Trial: The Clash of Medical Evidence and the Law in the Breast Implant Case* (New York: Norton, 1996).

7. For a conservative manifesto on this theme, see Steven J. Milloy,

Junk Science Judo: Self-Defense Against Health Scares and Scams (Washington, D.C.: Cato Institute, 2001).

8. Sheldon Rampton and John Stauber, *Trust Us, We're Experts: How Industry Manipulates Science and Gambles with Your Future* (New York: Tarcher/Putnam, 2001), p. 265.

9. Colin McMullan and John Eyles, "Risky Business: An Analysis of Claimsmaking in the Development of an Ontario Drinking Water Objective for Tritium," *Social Problems* 46 (1999): 294–311.

10. A number of recent commentaries have addressed the spinning process. See, for example, George Pitcher, *The Death of Spin* (Hoboken, N.J.: Wiley, 2003); Lynn Smith, "Putting a Spin on the Truth with Statistics and Studies," *Los Angeles Times,* June 6, 2001, p. E1.

11. D'Vera Cohn, "Married-With-Children Still Fading; Census Finds Americans Living Alone in 25% of Households," *Washington Post,* May 15, 2001, p. A1.

12. Compare Eric Schlosser, *Fast Food Nation: The Dark Side of the All-American Meal* (New York: Houghton Mifflin, 2001), pp. 239–243; and Douglas J. Besharov, "Growing Overweight and Obesity in America: The Potential Role of Federal Nutrition Programs," testimony before the U.S. Senate Committee on Agriculture, Nutrition, and Forestry (American Enterprise Institute, 2003).

13. Kathleen Maguire and Ann L. Pastore, eds., *Sourcebook of Criminal Justice Statistics, 2000* (Washington, D.C.: Bureau of Justice Statistics, 2001), p. 248.

14. The best overview of the competing estimates is Tom W. Smith, "The Muslim Population of the United States: The Methodology of Estimates," *Public Opinion Quarterly* 66 (2002): 404–417. For examples of the critiques offered by rivals in this debate, see Bill Broadway, "Number of U.S. Muslims Depends on Who's Counting," *Washington Post,* November 26, 2001, p. A1.

15. Calvin Goldscheider, "Are American Jews Vanishing Again?" *Contexts* 2 (Winter 2003), pp. 18–24. On the 2000 National Jewish Population Survey, see Daniel J. Wakin, "Survey of U.S. Jews Sees a Dip; Others Demur," *New York Times,* October 9, 2002, p. A23.

16. A growing literature provides various interpretations of the consequences of welfare reform. For overviews offering a range of viewpoints, see Douglas J. Besharov and Peter Germanis, "Welfare Reform—Four Years Later," *The Public Interest* 140 (2000): 17–35; Christopher Jencks, "Liberal Lessons from Welfare Reform," *The American Prospect* (Special Supplement, Summer 2002): A9–A12; and Sanford F. Schram and Joe Soss, "Success Stories: Welfare Reform, Policy Discourse, and the Politics of Research," *Annals of the American Academy of Political and Social Science* 577 (2001): 49–65.

17. Sam Dillon, "Report Finds Deep Poverty Is on the Rise," *New York Times,* April 30, 2003, p. A18.

INDEX

Median, 29–30
Medical errors, 67–69
Meta-analysis, 82–83
Missing children, 7–9, 46–47
Missing numbers, 1–25
Muslims, estimating population of, 159–62

Native Americans, 14–15
Numbers games, 125–30, 142–43

Official numbers, 103–13. *See also* Bureaucratic measures
Organizational numbers, 125–30. *See also* Bureaucratic measures

Peer review, 91–92
Percentages, 30–36; calculated the wrong way, 32–35; as measures of change, 35–36, 187n6
Pessimism, 88–89
Police shootings, 16
Population growth, 72–73
Pregnancy and alcohol, 55–57
Press releases, 95, 100, 102, 152
Probability, 76–78
Probability neglect, 83
Progress, 18
Psychiatrists, 104
Publication bias, 82

Racial categories, 14–16
Racial profiling, 137–42
Recession, 116–17
Recordkeeping, 103–13, 114
Relativism, 147–49

Religious affiliation, 13–14. *See also* Jews; Muslims
Replication, 82, 101, 114, 151–52
Reporting, 8–9; corporate, 128–29
Risks, 65, 74–87, 152–55; measuring, 79–83

Scandals, statistical, 113–14
Scary numbers, 63–90
Scholarly journals, 91–93, 95–96. See also *Journal of the American Medical Association*
Scholastic Aptitude Test, 121, 131. *See also* Educational testing
School ratings, 130–36; effect of school size on, 136
School shootings, 1–5
Science, fraud in, 93, 96. *See also* Junk science; Scientific research
Scientific research, 94–103, 148–51; funding for, 17, 95
Selectivity, 57–60
Sex, thinking about, 54–55
Sexual activity of high school students, 53–54
Smoking, 39–40, 74–75, 76, 81–82, 154–55
Sniper attack, risk of, 83
Social class, 134–35
Social construction, xiii, 146, 168, 173
Social problems, 64–67, 117–18; size of, 65, 67–69
Software, consequences of, 42, 46, 48–50, 52, 57, 172, 176
"Spinning," 155–58
Spuriousness, 38–40, 42, 80

COMPOSITOR: BookMatters, Berkeley
ILLUSTRATOR: Bill Nelson
TEXT: 11/15 Granjon
DISPLAY: Orator, Granjon
PRINTER AND BINDER: Thomson-Shore, Inc.